You Can Become A Super Salesman

You Can Become
A Super Salesman

By Paul R. Kenian

DRAKE PUBLISHERS INC.   NEW YORK

ISBN 87749-290-5

Published in 1972 by
Drake Publishers Inc.
381 Park Avenue South
New York, N.Y. 10016

Printed in the United States of America

TABLE OF CONTENTS

INTRODUCTION

There are always more selling jobs available than there are people to fill such jobs. A salesman or saleswoman need never be out of work. It is one of the few jobs where advancement depends directly on personal effort and not on the whim of an employer or supervising manager; it is one of the few jobs in which you can dictate your own hours of work; and it is one of the few jobs that leads to independence.

If there are so many jobs available for salespeople, then why aren't these jobs being filled immediately? The answers are simple. Most people have a completely false idea about selling. They envision a salesman as someone who speaks with authority, someone with a dynamic personality, someone who can override objections with great strength; this is just a lot of nonsense. There are many successful salespeople —people who make an excellent living year after year—who are modest, self-effacing, and who usually don't talk very much. If you never met these people at work, you would never know they were salespeople.

Is it difficult to get into selling? Not at all. As a matter of fact, unlike most other occupations, there are many employers who are more than willing to hire beginners. It is one of the few kinds of employment in which you can get on-the-job training and have an income at the same time.

There must be a hitch, somewhere! Perhaps selling is difficult. Actually, selling isn't at all difficult. What may be difficult is working your way up to the kind of selling you would most like to do. But here the final result will depend on yourself—your own ambition and determination. Many of our most successful salesmen never had more than a limited education. Some did not finish high school, and a few never even entered high school. In each case, however, ambition and determination overcame any possible obstacle presented by a limited education.

This is a practical book. Its purpose is to help you get a job in selling. It won't take you long to read it, but once you finish, you will know what is expected of you when you start your first sales day. Even more important, it will help you set goals for yourself in one of our most exciting professions.

PAUL R. KENIAN

WHAT IS SALESMANSHIP?

Salesmanship is the art of selling. We call it an art but it is also a profession, just as much a profession as being a lawyer, a doctor, or a teacher. Furthermore, salesmanship is just as important as these other occupations, for without it we wouldn't have our present standard of living. It takes salesmanship to move merchandise out of factories into homes. Without salesmanship the economy of the world—all business —would come to a stop. Salesmanship is not only a job in itself, it creates jobs for people.

TYPES OF SELLING JOBS

There are different kinds of salespeople just as there are different kinds of lawyers or doctors. A salesman could be a clerk behind the counter in a department store or the sales manager for a large corporation. The clerk and the sales manager both do the same job—selling. The big difference is in the way they sell, and how much they get paid for what they do.

Through salesmanship an individual can set his own goals. In selling, nothing can stop the man or woman who wants to get ahead, has the will-power to stick it out, and the ambition to rise to the top. There is no mystery about selling nor is there any magic formula; anybody can learn salesmanship. If you have the drive and the determination, you can become a successful salesman.

WHY SHOULD YOU GET INTO SELLING?

People get into selling because they want a job. Many people start in selling because it is probably one of the easiest kinds of jobs to get. The reason for this is that there are more selling jobs available than there are people to fill these jobs. As proof, just look in the help-wanted section of your own local newspaper. You'll find more jobs for salesmen and saleswomen than for any other occupation.

There is also another difference in the help-wanted ads for salespeople. For almost any other kind of job you will find a line reading "only experienced persons desired." For nearly any other kind of work, most employers want people with experience. These ads often specify special technical training, or demand high school or college graduates. These requirements, however, are often omitted from help-wanted ads for salesmen and saleswomen. Selling is one of the few jobs in which beginners are given an opportunity.

You Can Become A Super Salesman

WHAT IS SALESMANSHIP?

Salesmanship is the "art" of making somebody buy something. That something can be a product such as a television set, a tie, a dress, a farm implement, a house, or an auto. Whatever the product may be, if it is to move from the manufacturer to the buyer, it can only be done so through the help of a salesman.

Salesmanship means more than just selling products. The *sales item* can also be a service, or it can be an intangible such as insurance or education. When a sale is made, it does not necessarily mean the selling of a physical product—something you can touch or hold. Quite often a salesman will sell nothing more than a dream! A real-estate salesman selling lots in a subdivision doesn't sell land as much as he sells a vision of a house that is yet to be constructed.

Salesmanship also involves "selling yourself." An important factor in all selling is the relationship between you and your prospective buyer. Selling yourself means creating a feeling of trust and confidence between you and your customer. A customer may take home a product you are selling, but no product sells itself.

THE ART OF SELLING

Selling something to a customer—persuading a customer to buy—is what the "art" of selling is all about. Selling requires some skill, but this is just part of the total requirement. A salesman may develop a certain type of skill: a particular ability to handle words. A salesman may learn to appraise people, to learn almost immediately if they are "buyers" or "lookers," and so in a sense this is also a skill. However, this skill isn't enough, because selling also requires certain formulas.

IS SELLING DIFFICULT?

Selling isn't difficult, but, as in the case of many other professions, many people have the wrong idea of what salesmanship is all about. A salesman doesn't necessarily mean someone who is an orator, or someone with an extremely powerful personality. Some of the best salesmen say very little and most of them do not have an outstanding personality. Few of them could be called outstanding talkers, and generally, they do not speak any better or worse than average. Some of the best salesmen are unassuming people, have a limited vocabulary, and a limited education. Few of these salesmen fill the popular image of what a salesman should be. And yet, by knowing the art of salesmanship, they have achieved financial success and security.

In just one country alone—the United States—there are now more than five million people earning a living as salesmen or saleswomen. This may seem like a large number, but it still isn't enough to meet the demand. Because new goods are constantly being produced and because new ideas are constantly being developed, there is a continuing demand for salesmen and saleswomen.

HOW CAN YOU GET STARTED?

If you've never had any experience in selling, you can get *on-the-job training* and get paid for it. Selling in retail stores is an excellent way to get started on the way to a successful selling career and there are many job openings. This is particularly true for women; nearly half the retail selling force consists of women.

Some stores have *in-plant* training programs with scheduled classes one or two times a week for beginners. While much of the training time is taken up with matters that do not apply directly to selling—store policy, selling area maintenance, replenishing stock, record keeping—you will also learn how to greet customers, how to take care of their needs, and how to handle complaints. Some stores go further and explain how to close sales, how to distinguish between buyers and shoppers, and how to increase sales. Even if store selling doesn't appeal to you, consider the advantages of getting practical experience in selling. Some of the highest paid salesmen got their start through this type of selling work. They did more, however, than learn on the job, they also improved their abilities by watching other salesmen at work.

CREATING THE ART OF SALESMANSHIP

A salesman "sells himself" and in so doing, sells his product. It is because of this that a salesman must know himself, must consciously develop the skills that are essential to successful selling, and must learn something of human nature.

SPEAKING SKILLS

Nearly every profession has some basic tools. Words are the basic tools of the salesman or saleswoman. You do not need to be a college graduate to speak persuasively; when we say persuasively, we mean convincing someone to buy the product you are selling. A common misconception has the salesman cast in the role of a glib talker. Nothing could be further from the truth. Listen to a professional salesman and you will hear him using simple words, simple sentences, and, in some instances, doing very little talking.

What is Salesmanship?

How does a salesman speak? Naturally. A professional salesman always talks just as though he were engaged in casual conversation. Consider these practical suggestions:

1. Speak clearly. If the person you are selling to can't understand you, the sale is lost. If the customer has to spend any effort in trying to understand the salesman, then the customer has changed into a captive audience. Selling is an educational process. The salesman explains the value of his product; the customer takes in this information, but only if the salesman speaks clearly.

2. Speak naturally. A salesman isn't a college professor and should not assume he is one. Further, a customer will quickly resent being "talked down" to.

3. Don't rush. A sales professional isn't a "talking telegram." Make a conscious effort to talk a little more slowly than usual. Surprisingly, this isn't easy because most of us develop a rate of talking speed that is natural for us; however, conversational talking speed should not be the same as selling talking speed. Talking more slowly is also helpful for the salesman, for it gives him time to evaluate his customer, to speak smoothly without embarrassing halts or breaks, and to give the customer a chance to "break in"—to interrupt.

4. Don't use foul or profane language. Many customers are easily offended by filthy language, and religious or racial references. A customer may talk in any way he wishes; a salesman must use restraint.

5. Use simple language. Avoid long words—words with many syllables—when a simple word will do. If a customer doesn't understand what the salesman is saying, he is no longer a customer. Note the difference between a potential customer and an audience. A customer listens more carefully because he is

You Can Become A Super Salesman

involved. He may need to ask a question or answer one and so he is concerned with what the salesman is saying. A customer who lapses into the role of audience is no longer part of the selling process. It is this lack of involvement that makes him listen less carefully, or not to listen at all.

IMPROVING SPEAKING HABITS

Many of us do not speak clearly, don't pay enough attention to words, or have other careless speaking habits. This may be satisfactory for ordinary conversation, but not for selling. A successful salesman is always speech conscious. He keeps his thoughts well organized and makes a conscious effort to improve his speaking habits. The advantage of doing so means he is able to speak without "uh's" or "well, what I meant to say was", or other awkward interruptions. Again, this may be satisfactory for ordinary conversation, but these speech breaks can make a sales prospect think the salesman isn't quite sure of himself. Careless speech can lose sales.

MAKE YOUR VOICE LIVE

Many people speak in a dull, flat single tone. This monotonous and boring tone will defeat selling. A salesman is not only aware of the words he uses, but of the way he sounds. Just as words carry thoughts, so does the sound of the human voice convey feelings. A flat voice will give a prospective customer the impression that the salesman is not interested. If the salesman isn't interested, there is no reason why the customer should be.

On the other hand, successful salesmen can make even the simplest product seem irresistible with little tricks of speech. One of the most widely used techniques used by successful salesmen is to put heavy stress on important words. Important words in a sales pitch would include: substantial savings; large discount; limited time only; sale ends today; limited stock; only one to a customer; clearance. A successful salesman knows customer psychology and is aware that many customers want a bargain, are looking for a discount, and become impulse buyers when they hear statements such as "only one to a customer," or "substantial discount," or "sale ends today."

IMPROVING YOUR VOICE

It is almost impossible to know what we sound like, even though we may try to listen as we talk; however, there are two ways of checking. One of the best ways is to use a cassette recorder. These are available at a low price and represent a worthwhile investment for any prospective salesman.

To test your voice, insert a blank cassette into the unit and press the record button. Read from a newspaper or a magazine. If the recorder is equipped with a tone control, set it during playback for the kind of voice you think you have.

For women, the tone control should be set so that the reproduction is more in the treble range, and for men, in the bass range. A better check is to have a friend listen to your voice and then adjust the tone control for you. During playback of your recorded voice, try to keep these questions in mind:

1. Is speech too rapid?
2. Are words clearly pronounced?
3. Does voice sound monotonous, flat, uninteresting?
4. Are important words emphasized?

In the absence of a cassette recorder, enlist the help of a friend.

You Can Become A Super Salesman

Explain just what it is you are trying to accomplish. Again, read a short portion of a newspaper or magazine article and then try to get critical suggestions. Almost invariably, most people need to:

1. Speak more slowly.
2. Speak more clearly.
3. Vary the voice level.

YOUR VOCABULARY

There is a popular, but completely untrue, concept that salesmen are equipped with the "gift of gab," that they have an extensive vocabulary, that they are extremely persuasive, and that they do little except talk. Generally, salesmen talk only as much as required and encourage customers to talk. They may seem persuasive but that is only because they have learned the art of salesmanship. A competent salesman doesn't necessarily have an extensive vocabulary, but he is familiar with the words he uses, knows their meanings, and knows how to pronounce them.

To improve a selling vocabulary, avoid long words and words that people do not use in ordinary conversation. Avoid foreign words and words that are new to you. One of the best ways of doing this is to write a short selling speech about the product or service you are trying to sell. Then revise this sales speech by eliminating any unnecessary words and by substituting simple words for longer ones.

SELLING TRICKS

Every salesman or saleswoman usually manages to develop some techniques for increasing sales. One successful saleswoman of fine china

What is Salesmanship?

used to say to her customers: "I'm glad you picked that pattern. I was hoping you would. I'm trying to persuade my husband to let me buy it, but right now it's a little bit above my budget. I just hope they don't sell them all out."

Note the last sentence. This is a variation of the "limited stock" appeal mentioned a little earlier. The first few sentences of this saleswoman's approach are personal. They tell the customer:

1. I approve of your selection. It shows good taste. It is the kind of china I would pick for myself.
2. You are fortunate that you can afford it.
3. We don't have many in stock so now is the time to buy.

The few, choice sentences used by this saleswoman immediately established a good relationship between herself and the prospective customer. They took the sale out of the realm of pure, disinterested selling and made it more of a transaction between friends. The buyer-seller approach was changed into a woman-to-woman approach.

Still another successful saleswoman in the same china department used to tell her customers: "This is the last set we have in this pattern. I had it put away because I want this set for someone who will appreciate it. I think you're the kind of person that would."

If you analyze this selling approach with the one described previously, you will find that although they sound completely different, they are alike. The customer is complimented on her good taste; the customer is informed that the stock is limited. The important concept here is that one salesperson does not need to duplicate exactly the sales approach of another. Equally important is that each saleswoman spoke in her own way, naturally, but each conveyed identical ideas. These selling approaches, seemingly different, were worked out and thought out independently by the two saleswomen. The basis on which each saleswoman developed her selling technique is:

1. I want the customer to like me.
2. I want the customer to look on me as a friend.
3. I want to arouse a feeling of need—the desire to purchase—on the part of the customer.
4. I must be able to do all this in just a few simple sentences. Each sentence must be clear and readily understood.

It sounds easy, yet a good selling approach requires considerable thought, practice, and constant refinement.

SALES FORMULAS

A sales formula is a phrase, a group of words, a sentence or a group of sentences that have been tried, tested over and over again, and found to work successfully in selling. There are many formulas for selling. Every great salesman has his own pet formulas and books have been written around them; however, it is usually not possible to copy sales formulas directly, but only to adapt and to modify them. The reason for this is that duplicating someone else's sales approach, word for word, seldom works well. Words can be transferred from one person to another, but not someone's personality. A sales formula is a personal matter. What sounds natural spoken by one salesman will sound artificial and strained coming from another. Because no two salesmen can ever have the same personalities or the same individual characteristics, no two sales formulas can ever be the same.

THE SALES FORMULA VS. THE SALES APPROACH

A sales formula is a concept or an idea used in selling; the sales approach is the practical application of the sales formula. As an example,

What is Salesmanship?

one of the most famous of all formulas for selling is: "Don't sell the steak, sell the sizzle."

This is a formula, but it is not a sales approach. This formula tells us not to sell the product, but to sell its benefits. An automobile salesman doesn't sell a car; he sells status, or convenience, or convenient transportation. The salesman of television sets doesn't sell television sets; he sells enjoyment and relaxation. Manufacturers of cigarettes don't sell cigarettes; they sell good taste.

The "Don't sell the steak, sell the sizzle" formula can be applied to almost everything that is sold. However, the answer doesn't come automatically. Every salesman who wants to be successful must think about his product and then realize the benefits the product will yield. A typewriter salesman may be selling one of the world's finest typewriters: compact, unbreakable, inexpensive, and easy to use. While these words or phrases may be part of his selling technique, the emphasis will be on convenience (easier to use than a pen); speed (faster to use than pen or pencil); less writing fatigue; professional results. The salesman may emphasize the fact that a typewriter is essential to success in school or in business. The customer may examine the typewriter, be interested in its color or shape, but he is sold on its benefits.

LENGTH OF A SALES APPROACH

Selling isn't talking, although talking is part of selling. The ideal sales approach is one that uses the least amount of words but still results in a sale. A positive clue to a sales pitch that is too long is to have prospective customers walk away. Competent salesmen always watch their customer's body and facial movements to learn if they are talking too much. The prospective customer may look bored, he may start shaking his head or become restless, or may yawn; these are all signs of an excessively lengthy sales approach.

TALKING TIME

Talking time always seems shorter than listening time. Few customers are capable of concentrated, uninterrupted interest for more than a few minutes. Further, a sales approach isn't a monologue. No salesman can ever complete a sale doing all the talking, or even doing most of it. A sale isn't on its way to completion until the customer becomes involved and he only becomes involved by asking questions. A "solid" sales pitch, one that doesn't have a number of logical break points to allow the customer to join in, is self-defeating. A good sales pitch is one which encourages or prompts questions from the customer; it is one which is designed to draw the customer in and to make him part of the selling process.

THE MOST DANGEROUS WORD

There are certain words that help sales, while there are others that hinder or may prevent a sale. There are key words such as budget priced, discounted, manufacturer's closeout, White sales, overstock sale, new, latest model, improved, that should be part of any salesman's vocabulary. There are two ways in which to get a useful collection of these selling words or phrases. One technique is to listen to other salesmen and make a mental note of "selling" words. Another method is to look for them in newspaper and magazine advertising copy.

The most dangerous word any sales prospect can use is the word "no." Since this word means the end of any possible sale, the salesman's

What is Salesmanship?

technique should be to keep the prospect from using it. The method is simple. Never ask a question that could possibly lead to a no answer. Instead, remember the word "which." A professional salesman in a luggage shop will never ask a customer, "Do you like this luggage?" Instead he will say, "Which luggage do you prefer?" Note that the question is phrased to do three things for the salesman: 1. to keep the customer from saying no; 2. to involve the customer in a decision-making process; and 3. to bring the customer closer to a buying decision. A sales prospect cannot possibly answer no to a question that begins with the word which. No professional salesman will ever give a customer a choice between an item or nothing. The choice is always between one item or another.

IT'S THE LAST ONE IN STOCK

The thought that a product on sale may shortly be unavailable can cause some customers to buy. The danger here, however, is that it gives the customer a chance to say no. When a salesman says: "This is the last window ventilator we have in stock," in effect, he is saying: "Do you want this ventilator or not." This question could be answered with the word "no." The technique, then, is to emphasize a short supply without allowing the possibility of a no answer. In the case of the window ventilator sale just described, the salesman might say: "These two ventilators are such popular models, we may not be able to get delivery for some time. Which of these two do you prefer?" The word "which," combined with an indication of short supply, puts pressure on the customer to come to a decision.

You Can Become A Super Salesman

THE CUSTOMER'S DECISION

The preceding paragraph may indicate that pressure is being used as a selling tactic, but there are times when such a selling approach is necessary. The reason for this is that there are some people whose personal make-up is such that they cannot come to a decision. They prefer having decisions made for them. This type of customer is easy to recognize. They are often hesitant, shop intensely, and are often accompanied by a friend or friends to whom they appeal for advice. In a selling setup of this kind the customer often puts the salesman in the decision-making position. And if the salesman does not make the decision—if the salesman is reluctant to employ what is regarded as a pressure-selling method—then the sale will not be made. Note that with this type of customer there is no danger of a no answer because no is a decision word, just as yes is a decision word.

RECOGNIZING THE INDECISIVE CUSTOMER

The indecisive customer, accompanied by friends, will examine a large number of different styles or models, and will often confide in the salesman. They usually do not talk much, but they betray their lack of a decision-making ability when they do. They look for agreement, either from their friends or from the salesman. They are easy to approach and often confide in the salesman. A frequently used selling technique for this type of customer is to assume the sale has been made, after the customer has had sufficient time to talk about or to examine the product. This is done by taking out an order book and asking whether the customer would prefer paying cash or charging the item. Again, this is a "which" approach, but it also helps produce a positive customer reaction.

What is Salesmanship?

PERSONAL QUALITIES OF A SALESMAN

An item or product being sold is made up of two parts: the product itself and the salesperson. The way a salesman looks, the way he (or she) talks, dresses, moves, all combine to make up part of the sales package. It is true the customer may walk out of the door, possibly with the product under his arm, but an intangible part of that product is the personality of the salesman. In short, in selling, a salesman sells himself as well as the product.

But how does a salesman sell himself? This can be summed up in terms of three general headings: physical, mental, and ethical.

THE PHYSICAL ASPECT

More than the average individual, a salesman must be careful about his appearance. All salespeople, male or female, must be well-groomed. Just as gift wrapping adds to the attractiveness of a product, so too does being well-dressed add to the quality of selling. The reasoning is simple. Since a customer "buys" the salesman as well as the product, the salesman must present himself in as favorable a light as possible.

Customers are reluctant to buy from a sloppy salesman for several reasons. The first of these is personal. Put yourself in the customer's place. He feels the salesman has no respect for him or that the salesman is inferring he isn't worthy. He may even consider the salesman's sloppiness as insulting.

The other reason is that the customer quite correctly associates the salesman with the product. He reasons that if the salesman has no regard for his personal appearance, then he can have no pride in the product he is selling, therefore the product must be cheap, or shoddy. Included in this

You Can Become A Super Salesman

reason is the customer's not unnatural association of the product's guarantee or warranty with the salesman's appearance. In the mind of the customer the poor appearance of the salesman makes him suspicious of the validity of any warranty or guarantee.

A customer may look sloppy and may act that way sometimes, but a salesman may not. A customer's suit may be baggy and unpressed; a salesman must be well-dressed. There are no successful salesmen with a combination of dirty fingernails, chin stubble, unkempt hair, and an unpressed suit. The worst dressed customer will not buy from someone who is as badly dressed as he is.

Similar precautions apply to saleswomen. In addition, a saleswoman should be careful not to wear too much make-up or clothes that are too daring. In short, a salesperson should do whatever he or she can to make a clean, neat, conservative appearance—an appearance that will offend no one and will encourage the respect of all sales prospects.

THE LOOK OF SUCCESS

Some of the best salesmen sometimes go through an entire day, or a week, without having made a single sale. But you cannot know this by looking at them, nor can you determine this by talking to them. They look successful because their clothing and cleanliness shout success. And customers like to buy from such people. The "look of success" is another factor in successful selling.

PHYSICAL REQUIREMENTS

Few of us have ideal physical dimensions; some are too tall, too short, too thin, or too fat. While it is easy to change external appearances, it isn't that easy to change physical shape. But fat people can get thinner

What is Salesmanship?

by dieting, or, if they are unable to lose weight, can wear clothing that gives an impression or an appearance of slimness. Thin people can also gain weight by proper dieting, but can make an immediate weight gain through correct dress. But whatever a person's physical dimensions may be, there is always a way to make an improvement. All manufacturers try to make their products as attractive looking as possible. They know that such "window dressing" sells. For success in selling, follow the same philosophy.

MENTAL OUTLOOK

There are two ways in which a customer regards a salesman: by looking at the salesman's clothing, that is, the way he is dressed, and by looking at his face. A salesman may be well-groomed, but he may still act as a barrier between the customer and the product. Few of us are sufficiently "poker-faced" to keep our thoughts from reflecting in our facial expressions. A person who dislikes people looks that way because he thinks that way. The nature of a salesman is such—or should be—that he enjoys human contact, likes talking to people, finds selling a challenge, and each sale a source of satisfaction. If a professional salesman has personal problems, he is always enough of a professional to keep his private life and his business life separate.

ETHICAL OUTLOOK

The commonly accepted concept of a salesman—a glib, fast talking, high-pressure artist—may apply to a few, but the majority in the selling profession are human beings with the same hopes and aspirations as all

You Can Become A Super Salesman

other people. Since a salesman literally has to live with the item he sells, most prefer a product that can generate honest enthusiasm. They also know that a salesman who believes in his product is a better salesman. A professional salesman is also interested in learning as much as possible about the item (or items) he sells. He does so by:

1. examining the product
2. reading all the manufacturers' literature
3. talking to other salesmen about it
4. reading all advertisements about his product line
5. talking to service or repair departments whose job is product maintenance
6. getting "on hand" experience by using the product
7. listening to customers talking about the product
8. reading and studying competing products
9. thinking about the product

QUALITIES OF A PRODUCT

Before trying to sell a product, it is essential to learn its most important qualities. As an example, consider a cigarette lighter. What particular features would help a salesman sell this item? What particular features would help a salesman sell this item? Here is a representative list a prospective salesman might compose:

1. price
2. breakability
3. size
4. fuel capacity
5. ease of filling
6. striking mechanism

What is Salesmanship?

7. durability of wick
8. ease of replacing flint
9. design
10. guarantee
11. length of service
12. appearance
13. reputation
14. ability to light in the wind
15. kind of finish

This isn't a complete list but it does indicate the kind of thinking a salesman must apply to the product he wants to sell. Making a list, such as the one above, is an aid in learning as much about the product as possible. The advantage to the salesman is that he is ultimately able to answer all questions put to him by prospective customers, and is able to do so without hesitation. This leads to "selling confidence," an important personality characteristic of successful salesmen, because it shows itself in the manner and the way in which such a salesman speaks.

DOES IT ALWAYS APPLY?

While a cigarette lighter was chosen as a representative example, the same sort of thinking and pre-selling planning is applicable to other products. To be a successful salesman means knowing the product and knowing it in depth—actually becoming an expert.

THE MOMENT OF HESITATION

To the customer the salesman is an authority. The customer believes the salesman knows more about the product than anyone else. In effect, the customer places his trust in the salesman, and the fact that a salesman-customer relationship is established means that a condition of trust exists. But if a salesman is unable to answer a customer's questions, or if he hesitates or seems unsure of himself, then the condition of trust is breached and the customer-salesman relationship no longer exists.

But isn't it possible that a customer can ask a question that cannot be answered by a salesman? This can happen, particularly when a salesman first starts his career or when he takes on a new product. When this occurs, the important thing to remember is that the customer's trust must be maintained. All the salesman need do at this juncture is to admit not knowing the answer, but at the same time reassure the customer that he will supply him with the information required. It is almost impossible to anticipate all the questions a customer might ask. A professional salesman, however, will always make an effort to get an answer to satisfy the customer, and also to add the information to his own store of knowledge against the time when still another customer will ask the same question.

A SALESMAN'S CHARACTER TRAITS

The art of salesmanship involves the interplay of human character traits, some of which can be eliminated, while others may be strengthened. A shy salesman can learn to get over his shyness. At the other extreme, the overenthusiastic salesman can learn some restraint.

What are the important character traits that make a successful salesman? They include honesty, courage, sociability, enthusiasm, simplicity, sincerity, reliability, confidence, and ambition. Although this seems like a lot to ask of any individual, the importance of these desirable character traits lies in the relationship between a salesman and his

What is Salesmanship?

customers. A selling job becomes that much easier if a customer knows his salesman means what he says, that is, he is sincere. If a salesman makes a promise of a delivery date based upon a realistic judgment—a delivery time he knows will be fulfilled—and does not yield to demands for earlier delivery made by the customer, then the salesman will be regarded as reliable. If he makes a delivery promise, he wants to be able to keep it. It takes selling courage to adhere to a practical delivery date when pressure is exerted by the customer for an earlier time. A salesman is sociable in the sense that he enjoys meeting customers and likes to talk to them. Sociability does not mean being the life of the party, but rather the ease with which a salesman encourages the salesman-customer relationship.

WHAT'S NEXT?

Just as a teacher will specialize in a particular subject, or as a physician will specialize in one branch of medicine, so, too, do salesmen and saleswomen tend to go into a particular kind of selling. There are many different kinds of salespeople. Some work for a salary, while others work only on a commission basis. There are also some who get a salary and a commission. There are salespeople who sell products, while there are others who sell ideas only. There are salespeople who get a very modest income, while there are others who are among the highest paid in the nation. You will learn more about the different sales jobs starting with the next chapter.

SALESMANSHIP AND YOU

There are so many different kinds of salesmen it would be impossible to list them all. There is a great advantage in this for you, since it means there must be a place for your special abilities. It also means you can later develop one-of-a-kind selling so that your services will always be in demand. Another advantage is that there will always be a "selling place" where you can fit in most easily.

Don't try to make a decision in advance as to just what kind of a salesman you want to be. Salesmen will often move from one type of selling to another before reaching a final decision on the kind of selling they like best. There is more to this than just liking a job, although that's important, too. The fact is that a salesman who likes the particular kind of selling he is doing is a successful salesman. He doesn't have to be forced to sell, rather, he drives himself.

TYPES OF SALESMEN

To get an idea of the different categories of salespeople, consult the help-wanted section of your local newspaper. This will supply you with valuable information. It will give you some idea of the job market, it will let you know just what kind of selling jobs are most available. There may also be a job opening you would like to try.

When you consult the sales help section of the newspaper, you will begin to see some kind of job pattern emerging. You will note that some salespeople work indoors; others travel from door-to-door. Some are telephone salesmen who never see their customers; and some sell only by mail.

Some companies will hire salesmen and saleswomen and then give them an in-plant training course as an aid for handling their particular product line. There is no age limit in this kind of training, and you can often see young men and women sitting side-by-side with middle-aged groups in these specialty learning sessions. The factor that sets a super salesman apart from "order takers" is that the super salesman knows his education is never finished. He is always willing to learn.

There are five different kinds of basic selling jobs, but this is just a general classification. The five basic types of salesmen are: retail salesclerks; direct salesmen; wholesale salesmen; manufacturer's reps; and salesmen of intangibles. There are also some very highly specialized selling jobs; however, salesmen always start out in one of the five basic types. As an example, a salesman calling on physicians is known as a *detail man*. Such a salesman is not only characterized by his selling ability but by his extensive knowledge of drugs and medicine. A salesman of this kind might be someone who attended medical school for some time or who has had a large number of courses in chemistry and pharmacy. A printing salesman may have had some previous extensive experience working as a printer. But since you are basically interested in getting a start in selling, it is best to concentrate on the five basic types of selling jobs. These are the jobs that are most available.

EXPANDING YOUR FIELD OF INTEREST

Assume you want to start as a retail salesclerk. If you have never worked in selling, then this is an excellent first step. But does this mean that you could never move into a different kind of selling? Could you, for example, get a much higher paying job as a sales rep after having worked as a salesclerk? You not only could, but you would probably find your earlier experience a considerable advantage in your new job. No experience in selling is ever lost. Whatever experience you gain at a selling job will always be of help to you in more advanced selling positions. That is one of the great advantages of working in selling.

A good salesman can ordinarily move easily from one kind of selling job to another, quite often improving his take-home pay in the process. However, you should learn about the various kinds of salesmen as an aid in deciding which type of selling most appeals to you. Even if you start as a retail salesclerk, there is always the chance that you can move directly upward from that job to assistant sales manager, floor manager, or sales manager. In this kind of selling, promotion from the ranks is quite common. In other words, there are no limits to opportunities in selling. The only limit is the limit of ambition of the individual. If someone gets a job as a salesclerk, is satisfied with the job, enjoys its security and pay, and doesn't want any further responsibilities or challenges, then that person has reached the end of his own personal ambition. For someone who is more ambitious, there are many chances to move ahead and earn more money. One of the greatest advantages of starting in retail selling is that it puts you in direct contact with people who can open doors for you to better paying jobs.

RETAIL SALESCLERKS

A *retail salesclerk* is someone who works in a retail establishment, such as a department store, as a salesman or saleswoman. Retail salesclerks meet more people every day than people in any other type of selling. Salesclerks who work retail soon lose any shyness, learn to speak to people with confidence, have many chances for improving their selling techniques, learn quickly how to get along with others, and also develop confidence in their own abilities. This is quite a reward for a first job in selling. Many successful salesmen and saleswomen have started their careers in professional and profitable selling as retail salesclerks.

PAYMENT

How do retail salesclerks get paid?

Most retail salesclerks work on what is known as *straight salary.* This means they get a paycheck every week or every other week, depending on the payment system used in the store in which they work. To stimulate greater sales, however, many employers now offer an *override.*

WHAT IS AN OVERRIDE?

An override is a commission on what the clerk sells—a commission that is paid in addition to salary. Overrides are common in clothing stores

You Can Become A Super Salesman

and in stores that sell electrical appliances, radios, and television sets. The weekly salary is paid regardless of the number of sales. This salary, however, may be very modest at the start, but when supplemented by an overrrride it can result in a total that can be very impressive. An override stimulates the clerk's interest in the business, encourages him to learn more about it, and rewards his search for better selling techniques.

TYPES OF OVERRIDE

Some stores pay an override on all sales, while others pay on sales above a certain amount. The percentage of override will vary from one store to the next. Some stores do not pay overrides; others are generous. It all depends on the individual store selling policy. The main purpose of an override, though, is that it encourages a salesclerk to try to become a salesman, instead of being an ordinary order taker.

THE SEASONAL OVERRIDE

Some stores that do not usually have overrides may use the override system during a holiday season, such as Christmas, or when the store has a sale, such as a White sale in January.

An override, though, isn't something to which a salesclerk is automatically entitled. It is a sales stimulation policy set up by the owners of the store, or by the store manager. Just as a store has a right to institute an override, so, too, does it have the right to withdraw it. In some stores overrides are sometimes paid only on certain items. The purpose here may be to move particular merchandise that is either very profitable for the store or that the store may have in excess inventory. Sometimes a store will launch a sales campaign using newspaper and broadcast advertising, and will tie such a campaign in with an override for the selling staff, even though the items being sold may have been lowered in price for the sale. The purpose here is to encourage the public to come in and buy, with the thought that the buying will be extended to items not placed on special sale.

OVERRIDE RECORDS

If you work on an overall override, that is, an override that exists on all the sales you make, then you should keep a personal record of dollar amounts of total sales. However, your sales station may be so busy that keeping records is impossible. In that case you will have to rely on the honesty and accuracy of the store's records. Most stores will supply you with a sales slip book so that you will have access to your selling record. Then it will be easy enough to tally your sales to be sure you get the override to which you are entitled. Sales slips are numbered so it is easy to copy these numbers along with the sales dollar volume.

SPIFS

Generally, a retail salesclerk is responsible for selling a number of products. These may be similar items made by different manufacturers. Naturally, each manufacturer is anxious to have his product line sold in preference to all the others, or at least to have the salesman recommend his products above the others. To encourage salespeople to do just that, manufacturers sometimes offer cash inducements known as *spifs*. A spif is like an override in the sense that it is a cash payment. The difference is that an override is paid by the employer; the spif is paid by a product manufacturer.

Sometimes the offer of a spif is made directly to the salespeople

You Can Become A Super Salesman

involved, but more often it is made to the manager of the department in which you work. While a spif may sound like a pleasant way of producing more sales, it can produce problems, too. A store does not make the same amount of profit on every item it sells. Further, some merchandise moves faster than others, and although its profit margin may be lower, the turnover may be greater, and so the overall profit may be better.

Thus, there can be a conflict of interest between what is best for the store and what is best for the salesman. Therefore a salesman is sometimes faced with the problem of whether to push the items the store wants pushed, or those on which he will gain a spif. A spif, then, is a good way for a salesman to lose his job if he accepts it without managerial approval. It is a much better policy, and certainly more honest, to bring the matter immediately to the attention of your section manager. This doesn't mean the salesman will lose the spif, although there is always that possibility. But if you are the salesman and the spif is approved, you can at least accept it without worrying about getting caught.

Many large stores issue a set of guidelines for sales personnel, with the subject of spifs covered completely. Quite usually, salesmen who call on department store buyers are aware they are not allowed to approach retail salesclerks, but sometimes a "round the end" approach is tried, particularly with inexperienced salesclerks.

DISCOUNTS

As a sales employee, you will probably be entitled to what is known as an *employee* or *store discount*. This means your store will let you have the items you are selling, for your personal use, at a lower than retail price. The discount may range from as little as 10 percent to as much as

50 percent. But whatever it is, it is a personal fringe benefit supplied over and beyond compensation in the form of salary. It does not mean you are regularly entitled to buy merchandise at a discount for your friends or to engage in a little commercial selling of your own. The best way of handling the employee discount problem is to consult the store's employee instruction manual. If this topic isn't discussed there, then speak to your supervisor about it. It doesn't pay to jeopardize a job and a good future in selling just for the sake of being "nice" or doing a favor for someone, or to make a few extra dollars on the side. It just isn't worth the risk.

DIRECT SALESMEN

A person who works as a *direct salesman,* or saleswoman, has a job that is exactly opposite that of a retail salesclerk. The direct salesman works by going directly to the customer in his home or in his business. In retail selling, the customer comes to the place of sales, that is, the store; in direct selling, the salesman calls on the customer.

Direct selling may sound new and different but possibly that is because it is known under so many different names. It is sometimes called *in-home* selling, *door-to-door* selling, or *house-to-house* selling. In the United States, an organization known as the National Association of Direct Selling estimates that about one-half million men and another half million women sell merchandise worth many millions of dollars each year through direct selling. One of the largest cosmetic manufacturers in the world sells only by this method, using women and men to do door-to-door selling. An advantage of this kind of selling is that the direct salesman can set his own hours. Quite often, a direct salesman will start by calling on friends and relatives. While this is a very modest beginning,

You Can Become A Super Salesman

it has the advantage of supplying the beginning salesman with experience, and, equally important, with confidence. Another advantage of direct selling is that satisfied customers will often recommend other customers. In this way, the direct salesman builds a route of people who will buy on a regular basis.

WHAT CAN YOU SELL BY DIRECT SALES?

There are two ways of getting a job right away in selling: one is by working as a salesclerk in a store, the other is through direct sales. Each has its advantages and disadvantages. The retail salesclerk has a fixed salary. Payment for services is assured and there is always the possibility of earning extra money through commissions, if the store has such a policy. The disadvantage is that the starting salary is usually modest compared with other type of jobs. Also, the retail salesclerk has little to say about the kinds of products to be sold, and he is bound by the rules and regulations of the store.

The door-to-door salesman can select the products he sells, but works only on a commission basis. This means that income is not secure or insured, but it also means there is no ceiling on income.

Almost anything can be sold by direct selling, but the most common items are cosmetics, grooming aids, appliances, books, educational services, and magazines.

When a direct salesman sells to offices, his items could include office supplies, advertising specialties or printing. Direct selling also includes sales to stores, service stations, and similar types of businesses.

The items listed above for direct sales are just a few of the many that are possible for use in this kind of selling. Actually, any product sold in a store—and many that are not—can be used in direct sales. The important point is that you shouldn't get the impression that direct sales are limited.

COMBINED SELLING

Retail selling guarantees an insured income, and direct selling has unlimited possibilities; however, there is a way of having both. Some retail sales clerks pick up extra money by "moonlighting"—engaging in direct sales in their spare time. Aside from the extra cash earned, the experience is excellent for an ambitious sales clerk who wants to move up.

SINGLE SALES AND REPEAT SALES

A retail sales clerk may or may not be able to build up a loyal following of customers. It all depends on the salesman's store, its location, the kind of customers it attracts, and also on his personality. If, through your sales efforts, a number of customers are drawn to you, there are several benefits. The first is that each succeeding sale becomes easier. Your customer learns to rely on you and in some instances will insist on being waited on by you. The other benefit is that by building a following you become that much more valuable to the store. The general result is a higher income and other benefits, such as bonuses.

As a direct salesman, you will sell two general kinds of items: *single sales* and *repeat sales* items. A single sale item is one that isn't ordinarily ordered more than one time. This would include products such as vacuum cleaners, fire extinguishers, sewing machines, and encyclopedias.

A repeat sales item is one that needs to be ordered over and over again. Repeat sales items would include cosmetics, clothing, stationery, or any other object that wears out or becomes unfashionable. Repeat sales items are generally lower in cost than single sales items, although you will be able to find some exceptions. In repeat sales, though, the whole idea is to have a "captive" customer, someone on whom you can count as a steady source of selling income.

You Can Become A Super Salesman

There is nothing wrong, illegal or dishonest about this procedure. As a matter of fact, many customers prefer it for it gives them confidence in the product they are using. They also think, and correctly so, that as long as they are a steady customer, they will be treated with more consideration and courtesy.

Some direct salesmen like to sell repeat items because once they build up a following of satisfied customers, very little selling effort is necessary after the first sale. But there is a built-in danger here. The trouble is that the salesman may ultimately stop being a salesman and simply become an order taker. Again, there is nothing wrong with this approach. It simply means that this is as far as the salesman will go in his career. He has decided that this is the amount of income he wants, this is the easiest way to get it, and he will be satisfied with a nice, comfortable rut. Again, there is nothing wrong with this provided you know what you are doing and you are satisfied.

Some direct salesmen, however, prefer single sale items, because, as mentioned previously, these are often higher in price and therefore the selling commission is also higher. Salesmen of this type may also look on their work as a career or a profession, and may regard selling as a challenge to their ability. You will generally find this kind of salesman is one who has had considerable experience and has great confidence in his own ability in selling. This feeling of self-confidence isn't acquired overnight. You have to work for it.

THE CAPTIVE CUSTOMER

The modern trend in single sales is to move in the direction of repeat sales. The theory here—and it is a correct theory—is that it is much easier to sell to someone who has been a buyer at some earlier time.

As an example, consider the vacuum cleaner. This item is quite commonly sold on a door-to-door basis and is also sold in retail stores. At one time all vacuum cleaners came equipped with cloth bags that could be emptied by the housewife. Today, vacuum cleaners use disposable or "throw away" bags. When the bag is full of dirt, the housewife puts it away for disposal and replaces the old bag, generally made of some strong paper, with a brand-new one. In this way, the housewife becomes a repeat customer for replacement bags, and also for associated products. To hold on to their customers, each vacuum cleaner manufacturer produces replacement bags that are *not* interchangeable, that is, they can only be used in one type of vacuum cleaner and not in any other. In this way the manufacturer makes a "captive" of the customer. Further, when the vacuum cleaner needs to be replaced, the manufacturer, because of his contact with the customer through his replacement bag business, will most likely be the first choice for a sale.

Another example of the captive customer technique is in razor blades. Some razors will use only specific blades of a particular manufacturer. Once the customer buys the razor, he has no choice but to buy blades that will fit that particular razor.

DIRECT SALES PAY

Here is how direct salesmen get paid for their work.

A direct salesman will either work for a company or for himself. If you are planning a future as a direct salesman, you should know that when you work for a company you will be working on a direct commission basis. More simply stated this means that if you don't sell, you receive no earnings—no commissions. However, if you do sell, then the payment you will get can be substantial.

THE SPREAD CHECK

When involved in direct sales, the salesman or saleswoman will sometimes arrange to have part of their commissions deferred so they will, in effect, be receiving a weekly or a semi-monthly paycheck. If, then, some weeks pass by without sales, they will still have a steady income available. Some salespeople, on receiving a very large commission check, will have a tendency to overspend. They avoid this by arranging to have commissions spread over a period of weeks, hence the term *spread check*. A spread check is a commission check that is spread over a previously agreed upon period of time.

THE DELAYED COMMISSION

Sometimes, if a sale is a very substantial one, a company may pay a salesman his commission only after payment for the sale is made to the company by the customer. This means that the company employing the salesman will not pay out of its own funds but from money received from the customer. The advantage to the employer is quite obvious. The problem, though, is that it may be very difficult for a company to hold on to the services of a salesman if the salesman has to wait an unusually long period of time for his pay.

YOUR OWN SITUATION

The income of a direct salesman will depend entirely on the agreement he makes with the company he represents. If this is the kind of selling you want to do, then it will be important for you to have a clear-cut understanding with your employer. Experienced direct salesmen are in demand, and they often insist on an agreement in writing with payment terms clearly spelled out to avoid any possibility of a misunderstanding.

WORKING FOR YOURSELF

In direct selling you can be your own employer. You can make an arrangement, for example, with one or more manufacturers of various items to extend credit in the form of merchandise, which you will then try to sell.

The advantage in working for yourself is that your earnings can be greater. The disadvantages are that you may become involved with non-selling aspects, such as credit, collections, and shipping. But you may be able to arrange with the manufacturers you represent to *drop ship* for you. This means you will turn your orders over to the manufacturer, and he will not only ship the merchandise for you but may bill your customers also.

There is another great disadvantage in working for yourself as a direct salesman: you assume the credit risk because you are directly responsible for all goods shipped by the manufacturer. If the customer doesn't pay, then you will be asked to do so. Since you are placing the order, the manufacturer is under no obligation to make a credit check of your customer. In this kind of selling, then, you must not only be concerned with making a sale, but with whether someone will ever pay for the merchandise.

There are many kinds of direct salesmen. There are some who work for just one company, while others work for a number of different companies. Some companies have in-plant training programs for their direct salesmen; others do not. Some companies provide free samples and may even furnish a suitable carrying case for the samples. Other companies supply samples and cases but make a charge to be deducted from commissions. Still other companies charge for samples and cases, but absorb the charge if sales reach a certain amount.

THE QUOTA

Although a salesman may be working on a commission basis only, it costs a company money to carry him (or her) on their sales records. Quite often a company will not get an adequate return unless the salesman sells a certain amount. Many companies set up a *sales quota,* that is, the salesman must sell a certain amount within a specified period of time. Salesmen who fail to do so may have their services terminated, even though they may be bringing in a small amount of sales.

Sales quotas will vary from one geographical area to the next. A sales quota may be fairly large for an area that includes cities of substantial size and much smaller for less populated regions.

SELLING BY GEOGRAPHY

Direct salesmen in highly populated regions may often be able to call on a number of prospects throughout the day. In less populated areas, however, customers may be widely separated, which means the direct salesman may spend a considerable amount of time traveling from one account to another. Traveling expenses must then be considered as part of a salesman's overhead because these expenses usually come directly from his own pocket.

SALES LITERATURE

Literature describing a manufacturer's products is generally supplied without charge to the direct salesman. If the product is large or cannot be conveniently handled by the salesman, it is customary to show pictures in order to give the customer an idea of the item being sold.

THE WHOLESALE SALESMAN

What is a *wholesale salesman* and what does he do?

The wholesale salesman sells products in bulk to companies who either use these products in their own manufacturing plants or sell the products to their customers.

Wholesale salesmen often work for *wholesalers*. These are businesses that handle the products of various manufacturers. These wholesalers, in turn, may use a catalog to sell their products. Catalogs are books supplying pictures, descriptions, and prices of a manufacturer's product line.

CAN YOU GET A JOB AS A WHOLESALE SALESMAN?

Usually a wholesale salesman is someone who has:
1. Considerable prior experience in selling.

You Can Become A Super Salesman

2. A familiarity with the products supplied by a particular manufacturer.

If this sounds discouraging, consider that a student graduating from medical school doesn't walk into the nearest hospital demanding a job as a surgeon. There is the matter of previous experience to consider. The important point is this: *wholesale salesmen are made, not born.* They, like yourelf, had to begin at the bottom in selling.

WHAT IS A DRAW?

A wholesale salesman works on a base salary plus commissions or on a draw against commissions. This is an advance against what the wholesale salesman expects to earn. Note the difference between a draw and a spread check. With a spread check, the salesman receives commissions on sales he has already made. A draw against commissions is an advance against the possibility of making a sale.

As an example, let us say you are a wholesale salesman and you receive a certain amount of money from your employer every week. This is your draw against commissions and is a fixed amount, very much like a weekly or semi-monthly paycheck. If your total commissions are greater than this fixed amount, you will receive your weekly check plus any additional money you have earned in commissions.

If your sales produce less commissions than the amount you receive as your draw each week, you will still continue to receive the full amount of the draw. There must ultimately be a reckoning, however, and sooner or later you will be required to produce sales that will absorb all the advances represented by the weekly draw.

You should understand that if a salesman's commissions are consistently below the amount of his draw—the fixed amount he receives every week—it is most unlikely he will be retained by the company. Most often a company will only employ experienced salesmen on a draw basis, since some small amount of risk is involved for the company.

WHAT ARE THE ADVANTAŒS OF A DRAW?

The draw has a number of advantages for both the employer and the salesman. For the salesman, a draw is equivalent to a regular salary, so he is assured security. Also, additional sales can provide income over and above the regular draw, so the salesman has an excellent opportunity for greatly improving his take-home pay.

The value of a draw to a salesman depends on its amount and his own financial requirements. If the draw is so low as to be consistently below commissions, then obviously the draw has no real significance. For this reason, a draw is generally increased by the company if sales warrant it. Companies that have a realistic approach to selling realize that a draw must have some relationship to earnings, and that a high draw can act as a selling stimulus for a salesman.

Why should a company want to pay a wholesale salesman a draw against commissions? A manufacturer realizes that a good salesman must have his mind free of financial worries. If the salesman has any aptitude for his work, he will soon produce enough sales to more than justify the draw. The manufacturer has the advantage of paying salesmen what is, in effect, a salary, but what really does not load the payroll. The danger for the manufacturer is the employment of a salesman who consistently falls below his draw. In this case, an alert sales manager will either reduce the draw to be more in line with actual sales or try to stimulate the wholesale salesman to greater efforts.

A draw against sales isn't restricted to wholesale salesmen, but we are mentioning it at this time because it is so commonly used in connection with this kind of selling. A draw against commissions can be used, and is used, in many areas of selling.

MANUFACTURERS' REPRESENTATIVES

What are *manufacturers' representatives* (better known as *reps*) supposed to do and how do they get paid?

A rep is an independent business man who may have a number of salesmen working for him. A rep, either as an individual or as a business, contracts with a number of non-competing manufacturers and agrees to sell their products in a certain geographical area.

As an example, suppose you are a rep in the toy business. As a rep in this particular industry, you will sign exclusive contracts with various toy manufacturers, such as those who manufacture harmonicas, toy soldiers, trains, dolls, balloons, and boats. Note each of these toys is different and therefore can be considered non-competitive. Your contract guarantees that no one else can sell the manufacturer's products in your territory, and any sales in that territory will result in commissions to you. In other words, the manufacturer may not hire another rep to compete with you in the territory he has assigned to you.

As a rep you will be an independent salesman. You will be responsible for making calls on prospective customers in the territory that has been assigned to you. Your contract will not permit you to carry competing lines of products.

A manufacturer's rep pays his own expenses, including costs of travel, telephone charges, and any other payments that must be made in connection with selling the manufacturer's products.

OVER THE TRANSOM SALES

If the rep has a very large territory, he may only be able to call on his prospective customers once a month, or possibly even less. In such cases, the customer may mail his order directly to the manufacturer. Such orders are referred to as *over the transom* sales. The rep still receives his usual commissions for these sales since they originated in his territory.

On his part, the manufacturer will supply the rep with all the required sales literature. To help the rep get sales, the manufacturer may advertise his products in newspapers and magazines. Sometimes a form of cooperative advertising is used in which the customer and the manufacturer share the cost of advertising.

As in the case of other kinds of selling, a manufacturer may assign a sales quota to the rep. If the rep falls behind in his quota and does so consistently, the manufacturer may replace him with another rep. In turn, the rep may be dissatisfied with the manufacturer's product, or feel that it is priced either too high or too low. The rep may also believe that he is not supported with advertising or other sales aids. The whole point here is that an agreement between a manufacturer and a sales rep isn't permanent. It can be dissolved by either party upon proper notice according to the terms of the contract.

THE WORKING REP

Many reps work out of their homes, and sometimes set aside a room for use as an office. Each day they call on their *accounts* in an effort to stimulate sales, to listen to complaints, and to try to make adjustments to keep their customers content.

Some rep organizations are quite sizable companies. They may

You Can Become A Super Salesman

consist of one or more men or women who own the rep business and who employ salesmen to call on the accounts. The rep company is nothing more than a sales organization. The salesmen working for such a company may be employed on a salary basis, or, more usually, on a salary plus commission basis. In some instances, salesmen working for reps do so on a draw arrangement. Again, the whole point is that there is no fixed rule and generally each salesman works the best possible arrangement he can get for himself.

THE REP'S INCOME

How does a rep get paid? How much does he earn?

Many companies pay a rep on a monthly basis; however, there are some variations also. Some reps receive an accounting of their sales only four times a year. This means the rep must be able to finance himself for a three month period. During this time he must not only support himself and his family, but pay out-of-pocket expenses for transportation, meals, and so forth. Therefore, a rep in this position must have sufficient money to carry himself for at least a limited amount of time. The problem is not as severe as it sounds, however, for if a salesman reps a dozen different lines, he can ask to have payments arranged so that he receives income on a biweekly or at least a monthly basis.

There is a tremendous variation in the amount a rep can earn, but commonly a rep will get between 5 and 10 percent of the net amount of sales. Of course, some companies pay less than this. And in some specialized cases, reps can earn more than 10 percent, depending on the product sold, the size of the territory, and the need of the manufacturer for the rep. If the product is brand new and relatively unknown, and if the rep must really "open up" the territory for the manufacturer, it is quite likely the rep can demand and get a much higher than usual sales commission. On the other hand, if the product is well-known, if sales outlets are thoroughly established, and if the product is extensively advertised and in great demand, the rep may receive only 2 or 3 percent commission.

THE REP AND PRODUCT KNOWLEDGE

In some instances a rep may know as much as the manufacturer about a product. The customer may depend on the rep to supply him with information about the product—information that is not generally known or that is highly technical. An example is the manufacturer's rep who calls on physicians. Known as a detail man, the salesman must know more than the doctors he calls on concerning the medical products (drugs and medical equipment) he offers for sale.

OTHER DUTIES OF THE REP

A rep often has duties other than pure selling. He may be required to keep an inventory check for his customer. Thus, when he calls on a customer, he must be prepared to go over the stock, check to make sure no items are in short supply, and prepare an order for the customer's signature. The rep doesn't object to this because he regards it as a form of selling.

The rep must also take care of returns, that is, merchandise to be returned to the manufacturer for credit because of product damage or obsolescence. He must take care of any customer complaints, such as overcharges, wrong discounts, shipment of wrong merchandise, failure to ship on time, and so on.

You Can Become A Super Salesman

JOB POSSIBILITIES AS A REP

Can you become a manufacturer's rep?

Again, the answer is yes. The best way is to start as a rep working for some other rep. You can get this kind of job since you will be paid on a purely commission basis. This involves no risk to the rep employing you because he has everything to gain and nothing to lose, therefore the employment opportunities are good. Although you have no guarantee of income, at least you have the opportunity of acquiring some very desirable experience. In some cases, the rep organization employing you may even guarantee you a small salary while you go through an on-the-job training procedure.

YOU AND THE PRODUCTS YOU SELL

No matter what kind of selling job you get, one of the basic rules in selling is that you like the product you sell. Generally, women prefer to sell items such as cosmetics, while men tend more to appliances and hardware. This does not mean that a woman cannot be employed in a sales capacity in a hardware store and that a man should avoid selling cosmetics. But, if you are a male, and have absolutely no interest in hair lotions, face make-up, and facial tissues, then it would be difficult, if not impossible, to achieve success in selling. Since your customers would be women, you must also consider whether you enjoy selling to female customers. Similarly, if you are a woman and find yourself in appliance sales, consider whether this selling occupation is as desirable and as pleasant as it should be. Remember, the test is: "do I like the product I am selling?" The answer should be a "yes." If it is no, get into selling something else, for you are traveling a dead-end street.

Salesmanship and You

Select your field of sales. Don't apply for a job with a manufacturer's rep in the chemical field if you have no background in scientific or technical work, or if you regard chemistry as a dull, dry subject. As a salesman or saleswoman you can afford to be choosy, and that is exactly what you should do. Choose! And choose carefully, for your first selection may very well put your feet on a selling road that can lead to disaster or success.

Remember, selling is more than just calling on prospective customers and talking. You must know your products and you must know them better than the people to whom you sell. If you do not know your products, and know them thoroughly, you will not be able to build up customer confidence. You cannot really know a product unless you like it well enough to sell it.

SELLING INTANGIBLES

What is an intangible?

Mostly, *intangibles are services*. A prime example of the salesman in intangibles is the insurance salesman. He has very little to work with except ideas, therefore, his sales pitch must be more exciting, more vivid, more interest-holding than that of the salesman who has some product—something you can touch—to show. Salesmen who sell securities or advertising services also sell intangibles. A salesman of intangibles sells an idea or concept. He doesn't have a product he can demonstrate. This sort of selling requires experience, ability, imagination, and persuasiveness. Salesmen of intangibles are among the highest paid in the selling profession.

You Can Become A Super Salesman

HOW SALESMEN OF INTANGIBLES GET PAID

Because of the nature of the work, salesmen of intangibles are regarded (and must be) as the top professionals in the field of selling. They get paid in two ways: a salary, which is ordinarily high, plus commissions, or else they work on a straight commission basis.

Most salesmen of intangibles prefer straight commissions for two reasons: First, they have absolute confidence in their selling ability. Second, commissions are higher when there is no base salary. The result is that commission salesmen earn more money.

Salesmen and saleswomen of intangibles are often people who have had years of previous selling experience in other markets, and who are fully aware of their worth. Many organizations, such as insurance companies, have in-plant training divisions for the purpose of teaching potential salesmen. Tests are given by these companies to eliminate those people who could not succeed in selling intangibles.

SOME GUIDELINES FOR YOU

1. How can you tell which type of selling is best for you?
2. How can you find out if you are suited for retail selling or for working as a rep or for a job as a wholesale salesman?
3. What type of products should you sell?
4. Should you look for a selling job that provides a salary, or should you work on a commission basis, or both?

These are just a few of the questions you may be (and should be) asking yourself. It is better for you to challenge yourself at this time rather than at a later date, since your entire career as a professional salesman depends on it.

Salesmanship and You

One of the oldest of Greek maxims—a wise saying that has come down to us through the years—is "know thyself." This means you should know the kind of person you are. But why should you bother to know the kind of personality you have? There is a great advantage in doing so, for if you know yourself, you will be able to use your strong points most effectively, and you will be able to turn your weak points into advantages.

What has this to do with selling? What does the kind of person you are have to do with your future career as a salesman? The answer is that in choosing the kind of selling that is best for you, you must understand what kind of personality you have. You can then pick a branch of salesmanship in which your kind of personality has the best opportunity for success.

THE IMPORTANCE OF PERSONALITY

The success of any salesman, whether a retail sales clerk or a salesman of intangibles, depends on two prime factors—understanding himself and understanding his prospective customers. Understanding himself helps guide a salesman into the selling job best for him, and lets him concentrate on selling those products he enjoys selling. A salesman should also understand his customers. If he understands the personality of his customers he will know how to adapt himself to any particular selling condition.

Oddly enough, it may be easier for a salesman to recognize his customers' personalities rather than his own. Every successful salesman always analyzes the people to whom he sells, whether he does so consciously or not. It is much more difficult, although not less important, to be able to do some self-analysis.

You Can Become A Super Salesman

Just what kind of personality do you have?

There is no simple way of classifying personalities, but, in a very general way, all people can be grouped into three types of personalities. This classification stems from the work of a brilliant psychologist, Carl Gustav Jung. Here, then, is a description of the three types.

THE EXTROVERT

The word *extrovert* is based on a Latin word, meaning "to turn outward." The extrovert is a sociable, confident, jolly, outgoing person. He likes people. He likes to be with people. He is interested in everything around him. He likes action. He acts first, thinks afterward. Meditation, brooding, thinking without action— that's not for him. He makes quick decisions. He loves to talk. You will find him at parties, and when you do you will find him with a group of people. He is not a listener, and he is happy to have an audience. If he doesn't have an audience, he will do his best to collect one. He likes to attract attention. He doesn't mind if people talk about him and would be distressed if they did not. He likes to dress in the latest style, and the more "attention grabbing" the style is, the better he likes it. He is not shy. He has no hesitancy in introducing himself to others. If he has a business card, he passes it around freely. He generally talks somewhat louder than average. And while we have been referring to the extrovert as "he," women as well as men are extroverts. Being an extrovert is a matter of personality, not sex.

THE INTROVERT

The word *introvert* is based on a Latin word that means "to turn inward." The introvert is the opposite of the extrovert. He is anti-social,

Salesmanship and You

lacks self-confidence, tends to be moody. He is a withdrawn personality. He doesn't like to be with people too much. He likes thinking rather than action. He comes to decisions only after long periods of soul-searching. He is a quiet person who talks only when necessary. It may be difficult to get him to go to a party, but when he (or she) does go, you will find him off by himself in a corner somewhere. He dresses conservatively and will change his style of dress only after long and careful consideration. His clothing is generally subdued and neat. He is never without an umbrella at the slightest hint of rain. He is a reader and may subscribe to a number of magazines and newspapers. He is quiet, and when he speaks, does so in a lower than average tone of voice. And, as in the case of the extrovert, introverts are both male and female. Neither sex has a monopoly on this type of personality characteristic.

THE AMBIVERT

The introvert and the extrovert are extremes. No one is completely an introvert and no one is completely an extrovert. Therefore, an individual may have more of the characteristics of an introvert than an extrovert, or, on the other hand, an individual may be highly extroverted but still have a few of the characteristics of an introvert. It is this enormous number of possibilities that makes people so interesting. They are all so different!

It is quite rare for a person to be equally balanced between introversion and extroversion. Most of us are known as *ambiverts*—people who have both types of characteristics. We refer to people as extroverts, however, if they have mostly extrovert characteristics, and as introverts, if they have mostly introvert characteristics.

You Can Become A Super Salesman

THE EXTROVERT AT WORK

An extrovert, because of his outgoing characteristics, is often regarded as the ideal type for a selling career, but there are both advantages and disadvantages to being an extrovert in the selling profession. Here are some advantages:

The extrovert is an optimist and does not become easily discouraged. He is social and enjoys company. He makes friends easily. He asks for help when he needs it and will give help when asked. He adapts easily to any kind of company. He enjoys working with others as a team and obeys orders without objections.

Yes, an extrovert can make a good salesman, but only if his sales manager does the basic thinking for him, guides him, and makes him fill his selling goals. Under these conditions, his natural qualities of optimism and friendliness will be harnessed properly, and he will be able to move up to a higher income produced by his efforts in selling.

Some of the disadvantages are that the highly extroverted person does not persist in his efforts. He does not care about details. He seldom works in a methodical fashion. He dislikes manual labor (remember, some salesmen have to carry bulky, heavy sample cases). He rarely uses logic in his reasoning. He is impulsive and makes decisions without considering the risks or the effect his decisions may have on other people.

THE INTROVERT AT WORK

The highly introverted type of personality enjoys details. He likes to work his own way. He doesn't want other people telling him what to do. He enjoys thinking and planning ahead. He doesn't like to take risks or to gamble. If a job requires intense concentration, the introvert is the

Salesmanship and You

ideal type for it. Whenever his employer gives him an order or an idea, he will analyze it in detail before accepting it or working on it.

The introvert dislikes team work. He doesn't ask for help nor does he care to give help. He lives within himself. If he does make friends, they are usually other introverts.

It would seem that the introvert has so many negative characteristics that he could not possibly become a successful salesman, but this is not so. The introvert does have certain qualities that can be harnessed to produce selling success. These qualities are:

When he must, the introvert can act like an extrovert. Further, the introvert enjoys flattery and applause. The introvert has the ability to analyze a sales problem and to arrive at a solution. And so, even though the introvert doesn't particularly like people—and often doesn't like selling—he can be a competent and successful salesman when his employer praises him, let's him solve his own sales problems without too much guidance, and permits him to act like an extrovert.

THE AMBIVERT AT WORK

The ideal personality in sales would combine the best features of the extrovert and introvert. The salesman who likes people, is outward going, likes to talk, and who can think out a sales problem will undoubtedly be successful.

If you are a predominantly extroverted personality, you will do well in most branches of selling. You are most likely to succeed in retail sales and in direct selling.

If you are a predominantly introverted personality, you will be happier in selling that requires planning. This is true in selling intangibles or in working as a rep. It is also true, but to a lesser degree, of wholesale selling. However, these are generalizations and there are many

You Can Become A Super Salesman

exceptions. If you have the will, no matter what your basic personality, you can always strengthen your weak points and become anything you want to become.

Essentially introverted personalities, oddly enough, do occupy some of the top positions in the sales world, but not as salesmen—rather as sales managers. A sales manager must know how to sell, but he need not be a good salesman. He must know how to think, to plan, and to organize. Although many managers do rise from the ranks of salesmen, others get started by working in the sales department of a company.

THE TENDENCY TO OVERCLASSIFY

Although there are three basic personality types—the extrovert, the introvert, and the ambivert, this does not mean people can be neatly classified according to type. All people are different. No two persons have identical personalities. A professional salesman, though, regards selling as equivalent to understanding people, and makes every effort to do so. Selling, successful selling, is much more than just understanding a product or meeting a prospective customer. It means being a student of human nature, and this is something successful salesmen do successfully.

WHAT'S NEXT?

One of the questions people ask when they first think about getting into selling is, "How much will I make?" There are all sorts of financial arrangements between sales people and the companies they represent, so much so that it is difficult to say what is standard and what is not. In many

Salesmanship and You

cases a salesman must simply negotiate the best possible deal he can get. Keep in mind that a salesman—a good salesman—negotiates from a position of strength. Modern business cannot do without him.

HOW SALESMEN GET PAID

Salesmen, more than other type of workers, are concerned with the amount of money they earn. The reason for this is that the amount a salesman earns is often directly related to his own efforts. A man or woman working as a bookkeeper, for example, will get the same amount of pay whether they work energetically, or whether they move through their working day at a more leisurely pace. Not so the salesman. If he works hard, if he calls on one account after another, if he isn't stopped by weather or by rebuffs from prospective customers, if he refuses to admit discouragement, then he rightly feels he should be rewarded for his efforts. It would be a rare salesman who didn't calculate his commissions after making a sale, particularly after making a good sale. A good salesman will try to think of a dozen different ways of improving his sales, and if he does improve them, he feels he should earn more money—and he should.

In selling, possibly more than in other professions, income is directly related to effort. Also, much more than in other professions, the salesman knows he is working for himself, even if he is employed by a company.

HOW MUCH CAN A SALESMAN MAKE?

One of the great attractions of selling as a profession is the possibility of substantial returns, or, to put it more bluntly, the chance to make a lot of money. But an exceptional income is *not* guaranteed. However, every good salesman feels that his income, if not as large as it might be today, will be high at some future date and that his income will be due to his own efforts.

There is nothing wrong with this kind of thinking.

In selling, possibly more than in any other profession, the ability to earn depends upon an individual's own efforts. Since the majority of salesmen earn commissions, there is a high ceiling to potential income. Stated simply, the more a salesman sells, the more he earns. Does this mean all salesmen have approximately the same income? No, for in actual practice the income range is wide.

YOUR OWN EARNING POWER

But how does this concern you personally?

The potential amount of income may help you decide on the type of selling you want to do. For example, as a sales trainee or as a novice retail sales clerk, you will not be earning much. A sales clerk trades the risk of no earnings on a commission basis for security—the assurance of a

You Can Become A Super Salesman

weekly paycheck. On the other hand, a highly successful salesman of intangibles, such as insurance, can become one of the top income earners in the country. This doesn't mean that right at the beginning of your career you may decide to become a highly paid insurance salesman; it just doesn't work that way. Try to get some selling experience first. You will need quite a bit of lower level sales experience before moving ahead. The important point to remember is that there's always more room at the top. Although you may have to begin as a retail selling clerk or work door-to-door on a commission basis, your future isn't limited to these activities. If you are sufficiently ambitious, you can establish your own goals. Many people never advance because they never make any plans for the future.

METHODS OF PAYMENT

In general, salesmen are paid in one or more of six different ways:
1. Straight salary
2. Salary with an incentive bonus
3. Salary plus expenses
4. Drawing account against commissions
5. Drawing account plus expenses
6. Straight commissions

While these represent only six different categories, there are all sorts of possible combinations. Thus, number three item above shows salary plus expenses, but a salesman might get both, and also receive an override, or a bonus, or might get a small commission in addition to salary. Another fact to consider is that salesmen sometimes receive prizes for sales achievements. These prizes might consist of expensive gifts such as an automobile, or a trip to some resort with all expenses paid. Salesmen and

How Salesmen Get Paid

saleswomen commonly receive selling incentive awards such as watches or perfume. In other instances, a salesman may be given a company car for his own personal use, with gasoline and insurance provided by his company. Thus, the concept of how much a salesman earns cannot be only measured by using a weekly salary as a yardstick. The "side benefits" are sometimes quite valuable, and salesmen often come to look on them as part of the income to which they are entitled.

STRAIGHT SALARY

The kind of income that is best for you will be determined by your own needs. If you have no previous selling experience, and you have the responsibility of not only supporting yourself but a family as well, then a straight salary may be the best form of compensation. A straight salary offers the maximum security: It is regular, you can depend on it, and you know exactly how much money you will be getting at the end of each week or pay period.

Another advantage of a straight salary is that it will enable you to budget your income against your expenses, and so you can plan for weeks, even months, ahead. Finally, if you're switching to salesmanship from some other kind of work in which you've been accustomed to a straight salary, continuing that straight salary as a salesman or saleswoman will make the changeover from your old job to your new one a lot easier, both mentally and financially.

There is one big disadvantage of working for a straight salary in selling: The pay is usually low. While you do have the chance of moving up into a sales managerial position, you must also consider that every other sales person working on a salary may be in competition with you for that job.

You Can Become A Super Salesman

A salaried salesman is less independent than a salesman selling on a straight commission basis. From the viewpoint of the employer, a salaried salesman can be more easily replaced than a straight commission salesman. And so, the word "security" applies only to your weekly paycheck as long as you receive it.

A salaried salesman usually works indoors or in some fixed location, therefore his chances for new job opportunities are limited because he may not learn about them. A salesman working on a straight commission basis, however, is generally an "outside" man, and so has excellent opportunities for making new and important contacts. Furthermore, his employer is aware of this fact, and thus it is the employers who are in competition with each other for the services of a straight commission salesman. This condition is exactly the opposite of that of a salesman who works on a straight salary. In this case it is the employees—the straight salaried salesmen—who are in competition with each other.

BE REALISTIC ABOUT IT

Does this mean, then, that with these disadvantages, you should not consider working as a straight salary salesman? Not at all! It does mean that if you decide to take such a job, you should go into it with your eyes open, carefully weighing the advantages and disadvantages.

YOUR PERSONAL PROBLEMS

Let us say you have no choice in the matter and because of your responsibilities you must depend upon a weekly paycheck. First, don't worry too much about it, you have plenty of company. But when you do get a job in selling and do get a straight salary, you should not let yourself slip into a comfortable rut for two very good reasons: 1. Your income will never be very much; and 2. The day you reach the top of your pay bracket, your employer will seriously consider replacing you with a beginner at a lower salary. So, when you take such a job the first thing you should do is learn as much about the work as you possibly can. You won't be expected to make any great sales records so at least you will not have this pressure on you. If there are any "sales contests," do your best to improve your sales to get the benefit of any cash awards. The benefit (in addition to the extra money) is that you may be considered for a better selling position, or you may be offered a commission or override in addition to your salary. When this happens, you will be on your way to independence.

Secondly, if you get the opportunity to do some commission selling in your spare time, grab the chance. You may make little or no money, but that's not the point. The on-the-job experience will let you know whether you are indeed a salesman on the way up. Naturally, doing this in addition to your regular job is hard work.

TYPES OF JOBS

Most sales trainees and beginners in selling usually work on a straight salary basis. Other salaried jobs may include industrial salesmen (men who sell industrial products such as chemicals, metals, heavy machinery); building materials salesmen; textbook salesmen; retail salesmen. Men and women who work in retail establishments, such as department stores or smaller shops, usually work on a straight salary basis.

You Can Become A Super Salesman

These are just a few examples. All you need do is to read the help-wanted ads in your local newspaper or visit some of your local employment agencies, and you will soon learn of the type of jobs in selling with straight salaries.

STRAIGHT SALARY PLUS

The straight salary concept has any number of variations. After you have worked for a while on a straight salary, you may be offered a commission, in addition to salary, or a permanent bonus incentive, or special sales bonus. You may also be put on a quota basis. This means that even though you do work for a straight salary, you are expected to produce a minimum number of sales—enough to justify your salary. A quota arrangement has advantages and disadvantages. The disadvantage is that failure to reach the quota over a period of time often results in termination of the job. The advantage is that reaching the quota and selling beyond the quota may give you additional income plus the opportunity to move up to a better spot or to a better financial arrangement. If, by now, you have suspected that selling is competitive, you've reached a correct conclusion. Remember, though, you're competing with people, and they have the same anxieties, worries, frustrations, and doubts you have. Supersalesmen aren't born, they are made, and, they are self-made.

THE IN-PLANT TRAINING PROGRAM

If the company employing you as a straight salary salesman offers you the chance to learn under an in-plant training program, grab it. Some companies will give you time off for training purposes; others will insist that this be done on your own time. Don't quibble about it. If you attend, the fact that you are doing so will be entered in your record and will be in your favor when and if a promotional opportunity comes along. The teachers are generally salesmen with years of experience and they can and will be able to help you. Don't look on it as going back to school, instead, approach the in-plant training program with the right attitude: You are being handed opportunity on a silver platter.

SALARY WITH AN INCENTIVE BONUS

The override or commissions paid to salesmen and saleswomen are payments used to stimulate sales. Overrides, commissions, and bonuses are often made available to straight salary salesman, just as they are to other kinds of salesmen. The difference is that the override, or bonus, or commission paid to salaried salesmen are generally smaller than those paid to other type of salesmen, such as commission salesmen. The reason for this is the greater risk of commission vs. salaried salesmen. In addition, the incentive bonus you receive may not always be in cash. A company may offer a gift such as a television set or luggage, because the company may want to move some of these items out of their own inventory. Further, the company buys these items at a substantial discount, but generally quotes the full list price when offering them as "bonus gifts."

Again, if you are satisfied with a salary, then the bonus is of no great importance. If you do plan to make selling your career, however, the bonus is more than just a bonus. It's a challenge.

You Can Become A Super Salesman

SALARY INCREASES

There is still one more incentive a salaried salesman may have—salary increases. The man or woman who shows constant and consistent selling improvement is likely to get raises in pay. However, there are two disturbing factors here. The first, of course, is that the pay raises will be small because the original base pay is small. The second factor is that if you get paid more, you will be expected to sell more. Every salaried salesman must produce enough sales to justify 1. keeping him on the payroll, and 2. giving him a raise. An increase in pay doesn't always mean you are entitled to it. Your company may be testing to determine if more pay will give you more selling ambition. An increase in salary isn't always a pat on the back!

SALARY PLUS EXPENSES

In addition to the indoor type of salesman, there are also salespeople who "go on the road," that is, who do traveling for their company. The pay schedule for such traveling salesmen ranges all the way from full salary to commission only, with all sorts of possible combinations in between. In many cases, the company pays all traveling expenses. A list of a salesman's traveling costs is known as an *expense account.*

THE EXPENSE ACCOUNT

The expense account has been the source of much humor, and there have been many misconceptions concerning it. The most common idea is that a salesman can increase his income by "padding" his expense account. The truth of the matter is that any salesman who does this will soon find himself forced to look for other employment.

Company comptrollers—executives who control company finances—and company sales managers have definite standards of what a salesman should spend on food, shelter, and other expenses, and any attempt to pad an expense account will probably be detected. This is particularly true if the sales manager is a former traveling salesman himself. In that case he will, through personal experience, know fairly closely the amount of money to be spent on a selling trip. Further, the company keeps records of traveling expenses and over a period of time has learned rather accurately just what a trip should cost. The salesman who regards his expense account as an extra source of income is often astonished, when his services are terminated, to learn that his employer considers it as theft.

EXPENSE ACCOUNT RULES

There are no rules governing the way you should spend money on an expense account. Some companies, especially those concerned with their status, may actually encourage their traveling men to use the finest hotels, eat at the best restaurants, and spare no expense. Other companies may scrutinize each expenditure with the utmost care and caution the salesman against any free and easy spending. Each company sets its own expense policy—a policy the salesman should follow.

BENEFITS OF AN EXPENSE ACCOUNT

Does what we have said imply that a salesman cannot possibly benefit from an expense account? Not at all! There are many advantages: The salesman may stay at a quality hotel, which might normally be too expensive for his own personal travels. Some employers may prefer deluxe hotels, even if the cost to them is much greater, because this makes a better impression on customers if they have to contact the salesman for some reason. A salesman may also use his hotel room as his "display room" and so a room in a quality hotel is a selling advantage.

The salesman provided with an expense account may also use it to take his customers to dinner or to a show. If so, the dinner will usually be at a better grade restaurant, and the seats at the show may be better than those to which the salesman is personally accustomed.

The salesman working with the help of an expense account may travel by jet or by company car. He may be required and expected to rent a car to expedite his movements from one customer to another. Meals, normally paid for by the salesman while living at home, are usually considered a legitimate traveling expense account item by the employer.

All of these items we have mentioned are properly regarded as benefits by traveling salesmen—benefits to which they are entitled because of their job.

OTHER TRAVELING BENEFITS

There is still another important way in which the traveling salesman can benefit from his expense account. If he uses his own car while on company business, the company may agree to pay him a mileage charge, plus all service and repair costs. An "auto deal" often preferred by many salesmen, replaces the salesman's own car with a company car. Again, the company assumes all expenses, and the salesman's own car can then be used by his family. In effect, the salesman becomes a "two car family" but with the expenses of one of the cars assumed by his company.

How Salesmen Get Paid

Most car plans now reflect a more mature attitude on the part of the employer. Some companies permit a salesman to have a company car for his own personal use, driving the car at company expense. This is an important benefit.

THE USE OF CREDIT CARDS

At one time it was regarded as customary for traveling salesmen to pay their own way and to be reimbursed for traveling expenses at the end of a selling trip. This was often a serious financial burden on the salesman.

Today, traveling salesmen are supplied with a variety of credit cards. Credit cards can be used for renting cars, for air transportation, for obtaining cash when needed, for hotels, for meals, and for other services. This means the amount of outright cash expenditures on the part of the traveling salesman is kept to a minimum.

In some cases, credit cards are available without charge, while for others there is a nominal fee per year. The credit cards are supplied by the employer without charge to the traveling salesman and, bills incurred through the use of credit cards are sent directly to the employer. Credit cards must be regarded as cash. The credit card company and the salesman's employer must both be notified immediately if a credit card is lost or stolen.

Companies employing traveling salesmen prefer the use of credit cards for several reasons. An accurate record can be kept of expenses. The company is less dependent on salesmen for written records. Many companies also use credit card bills as proof of expenditures for tax purposes.

Finally, then, the expense account, when employed legitimately, does help the salesman financially and does permit him to enjoy a much higher than ordinary standard of living. Some salesmen regard traveling expenses as a selling inducement over and beyond their normal income.

ADVANTAGES AND DISADVANTAGES

Selling on the road has many advantages. It enables you to meet people; to make important contacts; and to live better. It is varied and interesting. Its disadvantages are that it may mean long periods of separation from your family and friends; lonely meals and lonely nights in strange places.

TRAVELING SALESMEN AND SALESWOMEN

At one time the job of a traveling salesman was fairly well limited to men only; however, this idea that only men can be employed as traveling salesmen is gradually changing, and more and more traveling jobs are becoming available to saleswomen. Whether or not a woman will be accepted for employment in this particular capacity depends on company policy, but more importantly, on the product being sold. Generally, men are preferred for industrial products such as chemicals, metals, equipment, or machinery. Women have excellent opportunities for selling cosmetics, home decorations, and ladies garments. Whether or not a woman will earn as much as a man in traveling sales depends on the product, the amount of sales, the commission, and company policy on male vs. female personnel. Where the traveling salesman works on a commission plus traveling expenses arrangement, women employed in a

How Salesmen Get Paid

traveling capacity often earn incomes comparable to or greater than men. When fixed salaries are paid, the salary for a woman can be and often is lower than that for a man. This is just a carryover from a traditional bias against women working in a traveling sales capacity and is gradually changing.

GETTING A JOB IN SELLING

The easiest job to get in selling is one in which you work only on a commission basis and get paid only if you make a sale. Another selling job that is fairly easy to obtain is that of a retail sales clerk. Quite often both of these type of jobs are available even for persons without experience. However, as a general rule, a company will not hire a traveling salesman or saleswoman without previous extensive experience. Sometimes a company will promote individuals from ''in-store'' work to traveling, particularly if they have shown sufficient interest and selling ability. However, once you do have experience as a traveling salesman or saleswoman, this area of work is then available to you from other employers as well.

DRAWING ACCOUNT AGAINST COMMISSIONS

In a selling job in which the pay arrangement is draw against commissions, the sales person does not earn a salary but is paid by receiving a fixed amount each week, which is based on a percentage of the selling price of the product or service being sold.

The income of a commission salesman is likely to change from week to week. There are a number of reasons for this. The demand for his

You Can Become A Super Salesman

product may be seasonal. Sometimes customers develop sales resistance, or may be looking around for a lower-priced competing product. Then again, customers may have excess inventory that must be cleared out before new orders are placed. A drop in sales may take place when the word gets around that a new model is being developed, or that some competing company is about to release a product with greater technological "advances." Whatever the reason may be, commission salesmen and commission saleswomen do not expect to be able to "pull in" the same number of selling orders week after week.

COMMISSIONS VS. DRAW

Note the difference between commissions, override, and draw. A commission is based directly on a percentage of dollar volume of sales. Ordinarily, the commission is based upon the gross price, that is, the full list price of the product. The reason for this is that the product may be sold at a variety of discounts. Sometimes a whole sliding scale of discounts is used, plus additional discounts made if the sale is paid within a specified period of time.

The maximum price is the gross or list price. The net price is the price the customer pays after taking all the discounts. The commission to the salesman, if based upon the gross price, is larger than if based on the net price.

Commission payments vary from one company to the next. They can be based upon gross or net sales; they can be payable a certain time after the sale is made; or they can be payable after payment is made for the product. But no matter what the arrangement may be, the salesman must wait to get paid. A draw, on the other hand, is a payment to the salesman in advance of commissions and chargeable against them. In effect, the

How Salesmen Get Paid

salesman is really borrowing his own money. His collateral is the sale. The draw is deducted from the commission when the commission becomes payable.

An override is also a commission, but it is a commission payable on top of a salary or on top of another commission. If a salesman receives a salary, he may get an additional income on all sales in the form of commission, or he may receive a commission if sales exceed a certain amount. An override can also be a commission on someone else's sales. As an example, a salesman may be the district sales manager for a particular territory. In addition to his regular income, which can be a salary or commission, or both, he also receives a commission on all sales made by the salesman in his territory. In effect, then, as a sales manager he receives the override for directing the activities of salesmen reporting to him.

If all this sounds as though there is no standardization for payments to salesmen, you are right, and most salesmen prefer it that way. A salesman is a businessman. He likes to feel free to negotiate the best possible rate of pay for himself, and if there are many different combinations of payment, then he has a precedent for his demands.

DRAWING ACCOUNT PLUS EXPENSES

Many commission salesmen are required to pay their own traveling and business expenses. This is particularly true when a drawing account is made available.

What is the best arrangement for the commission salesman?

It is best when his agreement calls for *both* a drawing account and payment of traveling expenses by the employer. Real-estate salesmen, machinery salesmen, toy salesmen, and other salesmen of this type frequently work on draw plus expenses; however, this combination is usually paid only to those salesmen who have established successful selling records in their field.

The amount of weekly draw against commissions varies widely and is usually negotiated between the employer and the salesman. A salesman with a record of achievement behind him will receive a larger draw than a salesman with limited experience. Few, if any, beginners are employed on a drawing account basis.

Does this mean the beginner cannot get a job as a commission salesman? No, because the risk of no income is carried by the salesman. Companies will hire beginners to work as commission salesmen if such beginners are willing to work on a commission basis only, with no draw against commissions and with all expenses assumed by the salesman. In this way the company assumes no risk.

It would appear that in a situation of this type the employer has all the advantages and the salesman has none; however, it is one way for a salesman to acquire needed experience. Learning selling in this manner is a sort of sink or swim arrangement, but if the beginner can manage to survive, if he has sufficient patience and determination, he can ultimately earn far more money than working as a retail sales clerk in a store.

For a commission salesman the initial effort to get sales can be difficult. The commission salesman must work harder to get started; must withstand rough going. If he succeeds, he can become an independent, well-paid businessman.

STRAIGHT COMMISSIONS

This is the area in which top-notch salesman operate. When a salesman knows the art of salesmanship, he doesn't worry about slumps and steady income. He wouldn't dream of working for a regular salary. Most competent salesmen prefer working on a commission basis for several reasons. Their annual earnings are much higher than straight salaried salesmen. In addition, working on a commission basis means a greater amount of independence. You should understand that a commission salesman who earns a high income also produces a high income for his employer. In such cases, it is the employer who worries about being able to hold the salesman. This is exactly opposite to the situation involving a salaried salesman.

COMMISSION SALES PAYMENTS

Commissions, as mentioned earlier, can be based on gross sales or net sales. The actual percentage to be paid to the commission salesman is a matter of negotiation between the salesman and his employer.

Before coming to an agreement on commissions, you must not only know whether it is the retail or wholesale price that is involved, but you must know the percentage in each case. In addition to these two factors, there are still a number of other considerations involved. If payment, for example, is made on the wholesale price, then you should know if this wholesale price is to remain fixed or if it will change in the near future, because when wholesale prices change, so do salesmen's commissions. Further, the employer may set a ceiling on wholesale prices solely for the purpose of calculating commissions, even though the wholesale price may have gone up as far as the customer is concerned.

Whether commission sales are based on gross or net dollar volume, you should understand whether your commissions are payable on receipt of the order or when the customer pays the manufacturer. Thus, your income depends on the kind of agreement you make with your employer.

If the commission salesman gets paid on receipt of order, and, at some later date, the retailer does not pay the manufacturer for the goods received, the commissions obtained on making this sale may be charged against the salesman. Quite often a manufacturer will hold the commission salesman responsible for the credit rating of the customer. In some instances, a manufacturer will refuse to fill an order obtained by a commission salesman, if the order comes from an account that is considered too risky.

KEEPING RECORDS

Getting paid as a commission salesman is not as simple as working on a straight salary. For this reason the commission salesman must keep good records. He must keep a record of every sale, the gross and/or net amount of the sale, the commission accruing, the promised delivery date, and the amounts of commissions received. To do otherwise or to depend on the bookkeeper or the accountant employed by the company can only lead to arguments and dissatisfaction. A commission salesman is a businessman, and, like all businessmen, he must keep records. It's part of his job.

THE FOLLOW THROUGH

There is still another difference between the salaried salesman and the commission salesman. In the case of the salaried salesman, his job is done when the sale is completed. From that point on, responsibility for

How Salesmen Get Paid

delivery of and payment for the merchandise that has been sold is the responsibility of the employer. A salaried salesman can make a sale to someone who will pay for the merchandise with a bad check, or who may not pay at all. The loss is taken by the employer, not the salesman. It is also the responsibility of the employer to deliver the merchandise and to make delivery on the promised date.

The salesman who works on a commission basis, however, must "follow through" on the order. This means he must see to it that the agreed upon shipping date is honored, and be sure his obligations to his customer are fully met. If he fails to do so, he may find it impossible to get a repeat order.

SELLING SERVICE

A commission salesman knows that in addition to selling his product line, he must sell service. He must agree on a delivery date at the time of the sale, and he must make this delivery date a realistic one, a date he knows his company can meet. This means the salesman must know the inventory situation of the company he represents, the amount of time they need to pack and ship, the amount of travel time normally required between his employer and the customer, and the usual sort of delays he might encounter. While it is tempting for salesmen to make all sorts of promises about delivery, a practical hard-headed commission salesman will try to get his customers to adhere to practical shipping and delivery terms, knowing he will be evaluated, not so much on his promises, as on his performance. A successful salesman is one who looks beyond the present "I-have-it-in-my-hands" order, to future orders. A selling career isn't made on a single sale, but on a succession of sales.

You Can Become A Super Salesman

THE DISSATISFIED CUSTOMER

Obviously, if a customer is dissatisfied, his resentment will be directed against the salesman who sold him the order, in this case, the commission salesman. A commission salesman, then, may find himself taking on some of the functions of management. Some commission salesmen resent this since it cuts down on their useful selling time, but many salesman follow through on orders since they know they must do so to get repeat business.

It is apparent that commission selling is the most powerful incentive a salesman can be offered. A salaried salesman, no matter how well-intentioned, is not likely to put forth his best efforts unless he receives additional inducements. But a commission salesman, with the greatest incentive in the world—making more money—will almost always have to "go all out." The more sales he makes, the harder he works, the more money he puts in his own pocket.

WHO DO THEY WORK FOR?

Commission salesmen work for companies, but sometimes they also work for themselves. When they work for companies, they have arrangements that provide for drawing accounts, expense accounts, and frequently the use of a company car.

This "total" arrangement is an ideal one. It means the commission salesman is able to take full advantage of his profession. But to reach the stage where a company will supply all these benefits often takes years of hard work, patience, determination, and concentration.

The salesman who makes the most money through a combination of commissions and other benefits is the salesman with a proven record of achievement. Does this mean that such salesmen "coast" when they reach the top? You will find that such men continue to work hard, for this is what is needed to remain on top. A salesman who works on commissions will not readily give up the rewards he has worked so hard to obtain.

THE SELF-EMPLOYED SALESMAN

There is one way in which the straight commission salesman can conceivably make more money than being employed by a company, and that is to work for himself. This is true even though being employed by a company may give him a number of important benefits.

A direct salesman, working for himself, receives no draw against commissions and no financial help of any sort. And while the amount of financing a direct salesman may need if he decides to go into business for himself may be small, it does involve a sum of money that must be invested to keep the self-employed selling business going.

Some of the expenses involved include items such as stationery, calling cards, phone calls, traveling expenses, and promotional items such as letters and advertising circulars.

It is true that manufacturers will sometimes provide the direct salesman with samples of their products, but there are instances in which the salesman must pay for the samples as well. Also, since the sample is not sold (often more than one is necessary) but is used for demonstration purposes, this is an expense in the same category as advertising and promotion. Manufacturers, however, represented by a direct salesman will supply printed literature about their products without cost.

There is still one other disadvantage of working for yourself, and it is quite a serious one. Assume a direct salesman has completed a sale. It does not follow that the customer will make immediate payment. In most cases, sales are made on a 30, 60, or 90 day basis. In some instances the customer may take 120 days to pay his bill, therefore it is possible that a long period of time will elapse before the salesman will see any money for his efforts.

How does this affect the direct salesman? It means that when he first starts in business for himself, he cannot expect income for some time. After he has become established, however, the problem of immediate payment is no longer as serious, since accrued commissions will be payable.

The reason for emphasizing the matter of income for the direct salesman is that a direct salesman, working for himself, may fail, not because he isn't competent as a salesman, but because he went into business with inadequate financing. Being overly optimistic about commission payments and unrealistic about income can force a star salesman into a much lower paying job.

Although there are disadvantages to being a self-employed direct salesman, there are also many advantages. A direct salesman can work as long as he likes, where he likes, and when he likes. His earnings from sales in the form of commissions are usually larger than the commissions of salesmen who work for companies. A self-employed direct salesman can get commissions that are higher than those earned by any other type of salesman.

When a direct salesman completes a sale, he sends the order for the merchandise to the manufacturer he represents. The billing, however, is done by the self-employed direct salesman. When he receives payment, he pays the manufacturer for the goods produced and keeps the rest. In making a sale, the direct salesman has the advantage of reducing the price of the items he sells, since he can afford to cut back into his commissions occasionally. Often by reducing the price of an item, he will make a sale

How Salesmen Get Paid

that otherwise could not have been made. This means that the direct salesman, working for himself, is in an excellent competitive position compared with other salesmen who do not have this selling advantage. For this reason, many buyers for companies prefer buying from self-employed direct salesmen, since there are more possibilities for "bargaining."

THE MANUFACTURER'S REP

The difference between a direct salesman and a manufacturer's rep is that the rep sells, takes orders, and then forwards these orders directly to the companies he represents. The rep, like the direct salesman, must wait for the customer to make payment before he gets paid. The rep does not do the billing; the company he represents does. This method is the opposite of the one used by the self-employed direct salesman, who handles his own billing. As a result, the manufacturer's rep is in no position to manipulate prices. He must use the pricing structure set up by the companies he represents. He may not offer his own set of discounts, something the direct salesman can do.

The manufacturer's rep has all of the financial problems of the direct salesman. The rep has offices, staff, and a weekly overhead to meet. He is running a full-fledged business.

To compensate for these expenses, his commissions may be high. A successful manufacturer's rep with a staff of good salesman covering an extensive and productive territory can earn a substantial income.

As mentioned earlier, some reps do not have offices but work out of their homes. Those who do so are generally smaller reps, and quite possibly have no salesmen working for them. It is a good way to start since it helps keep operating expenses at a minimum until the rep can earn enough in commissions to afford an office.

Since reps are assigned a specific selling territory by the manufacturers they represent, the rep receives commissions on all sales made in his territory, even though the order may have been sent by the customer directly to the manufacturer, with the rep not at all involved in the sale. Generally, a sales rep may represent from one or two manufacturers to as many as a dozen or more. As a matter of ethics and good business, a sales rep will not handle competing lines of merchandise.

Whether a person should be a direct salesman or a rep depends on his own selling or business inclinations. A rep does not assume financial responsibility for the sales he makes; a direct salesman does. The direct salesman earns a higher commission than a rep. A direct salesman may not necessarily have an assigned territory; a rep does. This means that the direct salesman has a greater geographical area in which to make sales; however, he must make the sale and not the manufacturer, so he does not get commissions on *over the transom* sales—orders that are sent directly to the manufacturer. A rep receives commissions on all sales made in his territory, whether or not he is involved in the sale.

While these are the general guidelines for direct salesmen and reps, there are all sorts of possible sales arrangements that can be made between direct salesmen or reps and the companies they represent. Thus, a direct salesman may have to share a certain territory with other direct salesmen. He may share financial responsibility for the sale with the manufacturer, or he may be able to call on the manufacturer's credit department for information about the credit of a potential customer. The commissions paid to direct salesmen and reps will vary from one company to the next. There are standard contract forms in existence for

How Salesmen Get Paid

both direct salesmen and reps; however, manufacturers, reps, or direct salesmen are not obliged to use such forms, for they can make any financial arrangements they wish. Thus, a company may try to restrict a direct salesman from making any "deals" with potential customers, that is, they will prohibit him from price cutting. They may even set the prices and the permitted discounts. In the case of a rep, they may show their displeasure if the rep takes on more lines than they think the rep can possibly handle. Their thinking in this case is that the rep will not have sufficient time left in which to sell their own products. Finally, even within the same company, a rep may receive different commissions on different products he sells for them. If the company has a very popular product that is in great demand, the rep may get a smaller commission than for products, made by the same company, that are newly introduced or have met with some sales resistance.

WHAT'S NEXT?

All successful salesmen and saleswomen work according to a selling plan, a technique that they devise *before* they ever try to make a sale. Retail sales clerks who stand behind a counter and who take care of "off the street" customers may work on a day-to-day selling basis without giving previous thought to making the most sales. However, even at this low level of selling, salesmen and saleswomen with ambition will realize that retail selling is just a first step, and that in order to earn more money and get a better selling job, they must improve their selling techniques. In the next chapter, then, you will read about the three steps to a sale.

THREE STEPS TO A SALE

There are just three steps to take from the time you meet your prospective customer to the moment when you make the sale. However, these three steps are giant ones in your selling career. Each one of these steps is somewhat involved, but once you learn them, you will always be able to use them for your own advantage.

By learning how to use these steps, you will be learning the basics of salesmanship. These steps, then, are the foundation on which your selling career will rest. However, remember salesmanship is an art. It is an art composed of your own personal skill, of formulas that have been tested and have been found to work, and, finally, of your own character and personality.

STEP 1: THE SALES PITCH

Exactly what is a *sales pitch?* A sales pitch isn't one thing, but a combination of things. It is the way in which you introduce your product, the way in which you call your customer's attention to it. But it is even more than that. By now, you should have become thoroughly acquainted with your product. You will not want to became embarrassed by a customer's questions that might reveal a lack of familiarity with the item you are selling.

Your sales pitch must include two important factors. First, you must be able to anticipate any objections made by your sales prospect. Second, you must have satisfactory answers to such objections. The time to think about these two factors is before you start the sale, not during the sale.

There is also one other item that concerns this approach. Since you will know the possible objections, you may be tempted to "cut the customer off" by supplying answers to objections before the customer has a chance to give them.

Don't do it!

Let your customer say what he has on his mind. Don't cut him off, don't cut him short, and don't try to anticipate what he is about to say. And when your customer does ask you a question, don't answer immediately, even though you know the answer perfectly. Pause for a second as though you had to think about it, and then give your answer with an air of confidence and sureness. Naturally, this could be called play acting, and perhaps it is, but as you continue your selling career, you will learn there is a sort of "ritual" about sales. The worst salesman in the world is one who suddenly decides he is going to be absolutely honest (even though he is perfectly human and normal at other times), and lay the facts right on the line, short, brisk, and to the point. The customer won't be impressed and he won't regard it as honest. He will feel insulted and will leave. In short, he is not being treated as a customer.

You Can Become A Super Salesman

A sale should not be a monologue. It isn't a speech with you as the orator and the customer as your captive audience. With luck, he might listen to you for about 20 seconds, and then he'll turn and walk away. A sale is a dialogue. Your customer talks and you talk. If the customer doesn't participate in the sale, then the answer is simple: There is no sale. And if there is no sale because of the way you handle your customer, then for this time at least you are not a salesman.

STEP 2: SALES PROSPECT'S REACTION

The sales prospect's reaction can be positive or negative. By positive, we mean the customer gives you some indication he might possibly make a purchase. By negative, we mean the customer shows by his mannerisms that he isn't interested. In most cases, you must be prepared for a negative reaction. This is true even though the customer wants to buy. He is simply asserting his natural, self-protective attitude. The customer may want to buy, is interested in buying, and needs the product you are selling, but isn't quite sure, is undecided, is afraid of making a mistake, is fearful of overspending, or anxious to get a bargain—there could be a dozen reasons. This means, then, that before you start to make a sale, you must be prepared for two alternative courses of action: what do you do if your customer shows he is not interested, what do you do if your customer shows that he has more than a casual interest in your product.

STEP 3: THE CLOSE

Although it may not seem so the *close* is sometimes the most difficult of the three steps. It means you must recognize the psychologically

Three Steps to a Sale

correct moment for getting the order. It means you must know when to stop talking and to get your customer to agree to purchase what you are selling. It means you must know how to avoid an "oversell" with the possible danger of losing the sale.

THE GUILTY BUYER

If you have a good product, if it is worth the price you are charging, and if a prospective buyer needs what you are selling, why should there have to be a dialogue? You show the product, the customer pays, and you hardly need exchange a word. Right? Wrong!

There are many different kinds of customers, but we can group them, somewhat roughly, under several headings. One of these is the *guilty buyer*. Some people simply cannot buy without having terrible feelings of guilt. For some repressed, psychological reason, they feel unworthy. They want the product you are selling, but do not feel they are entitled to it. They must be convinced, seemingly against their will. They will buy, however, because as you tell them more about the product, what it will do for them, its advantages, its competitive cost, they will gradually weaken. Initially, they come prepared to buy, but all they wanted in the first place was someone to give them a number of good reasons that they can use to overcome their guilt feelings.

How can you recognize the guilty buyer? A guilty buyer will often use key words or phrases that are a direct indication of his state of mind. These include: "I really shouldn't be buying this," or "it costs more than I expected to spend," or "I hadn't expected to buy anything." The buyer, though, wants to buy, but needs someone to whom he (or she) can transfer guilt feelings. If the salesman makes a convincing sales approach, then the customer feels as though he (or she) has been talked into buying the product by a persuasive salesman.

You Can Become A Super Salesman

The important fact is that a salesman must learn to interpret what the customer says. "I really shouldn't be buying this" means "I do want to buy it and I hope you know how to talk me into it." No customer will ever admit to having such thoughts, and may not have them, but they exist in the customer's mind nevertheless. A professional salesman listens and he tries to understand the meaning and significance behind what the customer is saying.

THE FEARFUL BUYER

You will also have buyers who are suspicious of salesmen. Don't let it bother you. They are also suspicious of lawyers, doctors, dentists, their fellow workers, and quite possibly the rest of the world. What are the *fearful buyers* afraid of? They are afraid of being cheated. Actually, it isn't the loss of money that worries them so much as the fact that they might appear "less smart" than others. Here you must build up a feeling of confidence in yourself and your product. Yes, your product is competitively priced. Yes, the product comes with a guarantee. Yes, the customer can try the product. Yes, the product comes in different sizes, shapes, colors, and so forth. Yes, the product has been used and tested by thousands and thousands of satisfied customers. Yes, the manufacturer will back the product 100 percent. Yes, the product has been selling for over 9 years. Naturally, not all of these "yeses" will apply to what you are selling, but you can develop enough "positive" or "yes" answers to satisfy the most fearful buyer.

It isn't too difficult to recognize the fearful buyer. A fearful buyer tries to keep as much distance between himself (or herself) and the salesman as possible. Such buyers often appear apprehensive, look around to see who is watching, but do listen very carefully to what a salesman tells them about the product. They want to be assured. They want to be positive they aren't making a mistake. What is required here is an air of confidence on the part of the salesman. The sales approach requires some references to the fact that the manufacturer has been in business for many years, is known for his integrity, and sells only on a money-back guarantee basis.

THE "I DARE YOU TO SELL ME" BUYER

This type is sometimes known as the *smart aleck* buyer. Don't let him bother you for he is an easy customer to sell. His attitude is motivated by lack of security. He isn't sure of himself and must constantly prove his worth to everyone. A salesman makes an ideal challenge. In this situation, the technique is to listen, and listen, and listen. Don't argue. Let yourself be impressed. What the customer is doing is selling himself, and if he wants to do your job for you, let him. You can always use your salesmanship on the next customer. If you can last long enough with this type of customer, he will gradually let you say a few things too, and then the one-sided speech making will turn into a dialogue, with both of you talking. As you both talk about the product, you will note that his "chip on the shoulder" attitude will gradually disappear. Not always, but often.

THE "KNOW-IT-ALL" BUYER

The *know-it-all* buyer knows more about the product you are selling than you do, and will tell you this at the beginning of the sale. This customer is the self-selling type, determined to do your work for you. Let him. You aren't a salesman because you want to prove how much smarter you are, but because you want to make a sale. Keep that objective in mind and the know-it-all buyer will nearly always mean a sure sale.

You Can Become A Super Salesman

THE IMPULSE BUYER

Some people buy on the spur of the moment, often making a purchase of something they originally had no intention of buying. *Impulse buyers* are those people who make a last moment purchase of some item placed near the cashier's table. This type of buyer is susceptible to the "it's the last one in stock" approach. The impulse buyer will often interrupt a salesman, indicating a complete readiness to make a purchase.

SELLING IS AN ART

Each of the three steps to a sale requires a special technique so that you may reach the next stage of the sale. But remember the one word description of salesmanship: It's an art. It is not a science in the sense that you can use formulas that are exact and always produce the same results every time they are used. It is true you can set up sales formulas for yourself, but don't consider them as inflexible. Adapt your sales formulas to each selling condition.

FLEXIBILITY IN SELLING

Be flexible in your selling.

This means you should remember that while your sales may be similar, they are not identical. How can they be? There are no two people who are exactly alike. Even identical twins will have different ideas about what they want to buy. Your sales formula—the approach you use in selling—may follow a pattern, but you must deviate from your sales formula as selling circumstances require. Your sales techniques must

Three Steps to a Sale

always be applied in terms of the special situations in which you find yourself. As an example, assume you have a sales pitch that takes about 15 minutes to develop before the customer will indicate his willingness to buy. You know it takes 15 minutes for the particular product you are selling because that is the average sales time. What do you do, then, with a customer who comes along, listens about five seconds, cuts you short with, "OK, I'll take it." Would you insist on continuing your sales pitch to fill out the remainder of the 15 minutes? The customer has already indicated he is in a hurry, he is sold, and he wants to move on. On the other hand, you could have a customer who may require 25 or 30 minutes, instead of 15. That is why a sales formula, a specialized selling technique you have developed, must be flexible.

MORE ABOUT YOUR SALES PITCH

What is the first requirement of your prospective customer?

Before you say it is the product you are selling, consider for a moment, and you will realize this isn't so. The first thing a customer wants, *any* customer, is information. He may see your product, examine it, and may even try it. That's not enough. Nearly always there will be questions. What does this mean? It means he has a need for information and is looking to you for answers. If these answers aren't satisfactory, the sale is lost. Some of the customer's questions might be: How much is it? Is it guaranteed? Does it come in different colors or sizes? Can I charge it? Will you take a check? Can I get a free home trial? When can it be delivered? Will you ship? Can I get it gift wrapped? Does it come with accessories? Is it the latest model? Why does it cost more than (name of a competitive brand)? Can I get it serviced? What do I do if it breaks down? Can I get spare parts?

You Can Become A Super Salesman

After selling the product for a few weeks you could probably make up a list of over one hundred questions. There is one thing you will notice, however, the same questions will be asked over and over again. After a while it will be a rare customer who asks a question you haven't heard before.

WHAT GOOD ARE QUESTIONS?

While the questions show the customer's need for information, they are valuable for you in two respects.

First, the questions may force you to look on the product in a new light. They may reveal that you don't know as much about the product as you thought you did. They will compel you to think about the product, to get answers, and in this way to learn more about the item you are selling.

Second, the questions will give you a strong clue as to the customer's state of mind about making a purchase. When a customer asks, "How soon can I get delivery," you can be certain the sale is completed.

WHAT ARE GOOD ANSWERS?

Your answers must be positive, not be vague or indefinite. If a customer asks, "Is the product guaranteed," you must not only be able to give positive assurance but add to your answer the number of years for which the guarantee is valid. Your answers must be stated in such a way that the customer is imbued with confidence. Your answers should convey this feeling: "Ask me any questions at all about the unit I'm selling, and I'll have the answer for you." Your replies must always be

Three Steps to a Sale

clear and unhesitating. If you wait too long with your answers, you will arouse a feeling of suspicion. At the same time, don't push your answer right on top of the question. Don't give the customer the impression you know all your answers by memory. If you are asked a question, you are supposed to think about it and then give the answer. This is what the customer expects, and this is what you must supply. If you don't know the answer to a question and you try to cover up by being vague or by trying to avoid the question, you will have aroused a feeling of suspicion and may lose the sale.

THE FOUR BASIC QUESTIONS

Nearly all of a customer's questions can be grouped into four main categories:
1. What are you selling?
2. What does it cost?
3. Why does he need it?
4. Why is your product better than others?

SOME BASIC SELLING FACTS

Although these questions appear in this order, this does not mean they will be asked in the same order. Quite often the first question will be, "What does it cost?" and this will be the question the sales prospect has foremost in mind. If, during the course of a sale, you can get past this first question with a response that satisfies the customer, you will be more than halfway to the conclusion of the sale.

You Can Become A Super Salesman

QUESTION FORM

The same question can be asked in many different ways, and so it will be up to you to be alert enough to recognize this. Consider the question "How much does it cost?" You may hear it as:

1. What will this set me back?
2. It looks very expensive.
3. I don't think I can afford it.
4. It looks out of the reach of my budget.
5. I don't make enough to pay for something like that.
6. Is it sold on the installment plan?
7. If I make a small down payment, can you hold it for me until (name of a holiday, or some other date)?

These statements and questions may not appear to be the same, but they are, and the question is still, "What will it cost?" Some people are reluctant to ask this question directly, others like to convey the impression they can buy anything they look at, even though their purchasing power is small. It does take experience to be able to spot a "How much does it cost" question, but every salesman learns them, because variations of the "How much does it cost" question are asked over and over again.

IMPROMPTU SELLING

Isn't it possible to have an impromptu sale, that is, a sale that requires very little selling and one in which everything you say and do is done automatically? The answer here is yes, it is possible to make such sales from time to time, but they will represent a small percentage of your total sales. Every salesman dreams of customers who will come in, will

Three Steps to a Sale

know all the answers, will not need to be convinced, and will order in large quantities. Further, some salesmen carry these fantasies into real life, and if you talk to them, as one salesman to another, they will insist:

1. They never prepare.
2. They know little or nothing about the product.
3. They were born lucky.
4. They "naturally" attract the best customers.
5. They are "natural" salesmen.
6. They inspire customers with confidence on sight.
7. People tend to like them.

All of these statements are complete nonsense. If you examine the backgrounds of such salesmen, you will find they have many long years of experience and that they have been selling the same product or related products during this entire time. Naturally, they do not need to prepare a new sales pitch every day. After selling for a large number of years, a sales pitch approaches perfection. The salesman knows the answer to every question. He can "size up" a customer in seconds, and usually, in less than a minute, will know if the customer is a shopper or buyer, if the customer has any serious intentions about buying, and how close the customer is to making a purchase. With years of experience behind him, the salesman does his thinking about the customer almost without conscious effort. To the highly experienced salesman his job is the easiest in the world. That's true, but it is also true of any other kind of job.

But you aren't an experienced salesman. You don't have many, many years of experience behind you. You don't have the ability, as yet, to size up a customer in seconds. And so you must take the list of seven statements spoken by the experienced salesman with reservations. They may be true, but they aren't true for you. They may become true for you some day, but not right now.

As far as you are concerned, you will need to develop your sales pitch, keep improving it, study the product you are selling, and regard each new customer as a challenge and a source of selling education. Yes, with experience you will modify your selling techniques, you will know the product better than anyone else, you will be able to size up customers at a glance. Also, with experience you will know all of the questions your customers will ask, and so the need for advance preparation will no longer exist. You will then be in a position to tell beginners that you never prepare, that you don't study the product, and so on.

HOW TO ANSWER A CUSTOMER'S OBJECTIONS

Consider the two basic reasons why a customer may object to purchasing a product:

First, he thinks he does not need or does not want the product or service you are selling.

Second, he may want your product or service, but he wants you to convince him so that his own personal opinion of your product or service will be confirmed.

THE VALUE OF A CUSTOMER'S QUESTIONS

But how can you know just what a customer has in mind? In most cases you will be able to tell in two ways: 1. the attitude of the customer, and 2. the way in which he phrases his questions. As an example, say you are a bicycle salesman working in a store and are approached by a customer. His first words might be: "I've been thinking about getting a bicycle."

Note that the customer did not say he wants a bicycle, nor did he

Three Steps to a Sale

specify any particular brand. He isn't even sure he wants a bicycle. He isn't even certain he needs one. This is one of the objections we mentioned earlier—the objection in which the customer isn't sure he really needs or wants what you are selling.

Now let's consider your next customer. He approaches you and says: "Do you carry the Mark IV bike with three-gear drive?"

Compare this opening question with that of the earlier customer. Wouldn't you agree that the second customer has been thinking about getting a bicycle for some time? How do we know? We know by the way in which the customer phrased his question. He not only wants a bicycle, but he wants the bicycle of a certain manufacturer, and he wants a certain model. He has already made up his mind to buy a bicycle with certain features. If that is the case, what is left? What does the customer want? All he wants now is to be confirmed in his own opinion.

LISTEN!

A good salesman is one who knows how to listen and when to listen. As an example, consider the two customers for bicycles and their completely different opening statements. Wouldn't you agree that the two customers are entirely different? But how do we know—by listening.

The ability to listen is an important characteristic of a good salesman. Note we did not say to "hear" what the customer said. There's a big difference. By listening we mean not only hearing the words, but thinking about them, and using them to appraise the customer's needs. To have a good sales approach, or sales pitch, you must listen to the customer.

A sales approach that might be perfectly valid for one customer could be completely wrong for another.

You Can Become A Super Salesman

HOW OFTEN MUST YOU CHANGE
YOUR SELLING TECHNIQUE?

Does this mean you must have a completely new sales pitch for each and every customer? Of course not. It simply means you must adapt your sales pitch for each customer. In a way, though, doesn't this really make a lot of sense? After all, all people are individuals in their own right, and so all we are asking you to do is to recognize them as such. If you do this, your customer will appreciate the way he is being treated and will react accordingly. And if you do not, the customer may develop a sense of resentment, without knowing why he does so.

Therefore, while you must develop a basic sales pitch, it must also be flexible enough so you can adapt it to each and every customer.

THE BASIC SALES PITCH

Every sales pitch contains basic elements:
1. Greeting the customer
2. Listening to the customer's opening questions or statements
3. Answering the customer
4. Listening to the customer's objections
5. Answering the customer
6. Listening to the customer's objections
7. Answering and directing the sale toward its conclusion
8. Concluding the sale

Of course, this is a "bare bones" outline, but essentially it consists of questions and answers. During this time you not only supply information, but convincing statements in favor of your product. During this time you learn of the customer's needs, and try to satisfy them. During this time you listen to objections, and you overcome them. And all during this time, you not only listen to the customer, you look at him. You can learn quite a lot from the customer's facial expressions.

The preparation of a sales pitch should be built around two frameworks. First, the answers to the four basic questions, and second, the answers to objections you anticipate the customer will make.

THE BEST ANSWER

A customer's questions can be answered in various ways, but there is always one answer that is best. It's the one that channels a sale directly toward its conclusion. It is the answer that convinces your customer. You should give the prospective buyer the conclusion that the item he is buying will best satisfy his needs, that the price is right, that the quality is equal to or superior to the quality he wants, and that the item has all the features he expected.

REASONS FOR A CUSTOMER'S OBJECTIONS

Psychologists in business have made studies of the objections that prospective customers make about certain products. Every salesman should keep in mind that objections are made because of one or more of the following reasons:
1. ignorance
2. fear

3. habit
4. desire to postpone

EVALUATING OBJECTIONS

These four basic objections can, either singly or in a group, cause the loss of a sale. It is therefore necessary to find out if the customer is making a valid or true objection, or if he is merely making an excuse for not buying the article. Remember, also, that many people make inquiries about a product or try to give the impression they are possible customers, but they actually have no interest in what you may be selling. Retired people, unemployed people, habitual shoppers, elderly people, people who have time on their hands, often feel no compunction about using a salesman's time. They may have neither the money nor the intention of buying and may simply be shopping as a means of amusement or social contact. It costs them nothing, their conversation is solicited, they are made to feel important. You will not only find "false shoppers" in stores, but will come across them in any other kind of selling activity. For example, it is not at all unlikely that a buyer for a company will keep one or more salesmen waiting in an outer room just to boost his own ego and self-importance.

The non-shopper presents two dangers to the salesman. If a salesman is working on commission only or on salary plus commission, the loss of time spent with the non-buyer is the same as a loss of earning power. Also, if the salesman is unable to recognize the non-buyer for what he really is, then the loss of the sale (for there will be no sale) can be depressing and can adversely affect the salesman's attitude. As a salesman, then, you must learn to spot these non-buyers—those people who look on shopping as a form of free entertainment.

Three Steps to a Sale

TYPES OF OBJECTIONS

What sort of objections will a customer have?

We imagine you think they are limitless and there could be no way to describe them all. Actually, there is no need to do this, for all customers' objections can be put under two main headings: objective and subjective.

Objective refers to the object or article or service you are trying to sell. If, for example, you are selling automobiles, an objective objection would be one that concerns the particular automobile you are trying to sell. Typical objections would be: I don't like the color. The car is too large. It doesn't have enough trunk space. I wanted a more powerful engine.

Note that all of these objections deal directly with the item being sold.

The word *subjective*, on the other hand, does not refer to the article or service you are trying to sell—it does concern the psychological state of mind of the customer. Statements such as: "I can't possibly afford it," "I don't know where I would put it," "I really hadn't expected to buy it," "I'm just shopping around," do not refer to the object being sold; they are indicative of the customer's state of mind.

OBJECTIVE OBJECTIONS

We supplied you with a few objective objections—objections concerned with the product you are selling. We are going to give you a longer list now for the simple reason that you will come across them often in your selling career. By examining these objections at this time, by becoming familiar with them, you will be able to apply them to the product you are selling. In doing so, you will start to think of answers that will satisfy a customer's objections.

You Can Become A Super Salesman

Typical objections of the objective type are:

1. It's too fancy for me.
2. It looks much too plain.
3. It's not a good brand.
4. I never heard of this brand before.
5. It's not advertised.
6. Your competitor's product is better.
7. It turns dark or dirty as you use it.
8. It breaks too easily.
9. It looks too heavy (or too light, or too big, or too small).
10. It's not convenient to use.
11. I wouldn't know where to store it.
12. It's too hard to clean.
13. It's old fashioned.
14. My neighbors all use a different product.
15. I don't like the finish.
16. The quality looks poor.
17. I don't like the styling.
18. How do I know it will work properly?
19. A friend of mine bought one and he didn't like it.
20. There are better products available.
21. It isn't what I need.

This isn't a complete list of objections, but if you will examine them carefully, you will see there are repeats in the list. Actually, all of these objections can be put into four basic categories. These are price, quality, style, and features.

Now let's examine some of the objections based on price:

1. It's too expensive.
2. I can't afford it.
3. It exceeds my budget.

Three Steps to a Sale

4. I wanted to spend less.

5. I wasn't planning on spending so much right now.

6. I thought it was cheaper.

7. I don't have enough money with me.

8. I don't want to take on such a big expense.

9. I'll buy it when I get paid.

10. I'll buy it when I get my raise.

11. I can get it for less elsewhere.

12. Your competitor's products are less expensive.

13. Brand X is much cheaper,

14. Why did they go up in price? They were cheaper last week.

15. I want to do some comparison shopping first.

16. I can buy it elsewhere at a discount.

Right at the start you will think of these as very difficult objections. How is it possible to answer these objections when there are so many of them?

Go over each of these objections, read them carefully, and you will soon see a pattern emerging. While they may be worded differently, they all have the same basic idea. One customer might call the item you are selling too expensive, while another customer will say he cannot afford it; they are different words but they have the same meaning. Although these are two objections worded completely differently, the advantage is that they really form only one objection and so you need develop one answer.

HOW TO OVERCOME THE PRICE OBJECTION

The price objection is common in all kinds of selling. Sooner or later, and most often sooner, the customer will want to know how much he is expected to pay for the product or service you are selling. It is at this time that the objections based on price will begin. And, of course, you

You Can Become A Super Salesman

must be prepared to answers these objections. As an example, assume you are selling an item for $50 and a leading competitor has a similar item that sells for $45. How can you overcome what may appear to be a very serious objection?

OVERCOMING THE PRICE FACTOR

The first thing to remember is that many people equate quality with price. If two items are for sale, and one has a higher price than the other, many people will ordinarily regard the higher-priced item as the better one, when, in fact, both may be of equal quality. Even though they may object to the higher price, they will prefer the higher-priced item because they think it is better.

The higher priced item also has snob appeal. There are some people who will buy higher-priced items simply because it makes them feel superior to those who cannot afford it. A first class seat on a plane costs more than coach, but travelers in first-class can't get to their destination any faster than those in the coach section. Yes, they may get more food, free drinks, and are less crowded, but the basic sale is transportation.

There are other ways of overcoming the price factor. Remind your customer that the first cost is not the final cost. A cheaper item can be much more costly in the long run. It may not last as long. It may need repairs sooner. It may need an earlier replacement. It may not look as good as a competing product. You must know your own product line thoroughly and be familiar with competing products.

WHEN SHOULD YOU ANSWER THE PRICE OBJECTION?

If the customer does *not* raise an objection to price, *don't* try to convince him that the price is right. There are some customers who will

Three Steps to a Sale

be ready, willing, and able to pay, and you will only annoy them or arouse their suspicions if you start answering an objection that wasn't raised by them in the first place. Also, never mention the lower price of any competing product unless this is a point first mentioned by the customer. There are a number of reasons for this. First, your customer may not be aware that there is a lower-priced competing product. It isn't your job or your duty to sell a competing item. Also, there are some people who buy on a "price only" basis, that is, if two comparable items are being sold, they will always buy the lower-priced product.

THE BASIC DIFFERENCES

Just because a customer wants to know the price of what you are selling does not mean he is going to object. He must know the price, if the sales transaction is to be completed. And so, there is a big difference between asking the price and making a price objection. One is a request for information; the other is a mental factor of the buyer's that must be overcome. You can disregard neither: you must furnish the price, and you must satisfy the price objection.

SUBJECTIVE OBJECTIONS

Now that you have some idea of the objective objections, consider the other type—subjective objections. These objections have nothing to do with the product itself, but refer to some kind of mental attitude on the part of the purchaser. There are two ways to determine the mental attitude of your customer: through his questions and facial gestures.

Here are some representative subjective objections you will hear. They all have one thing in common—a desire to end the dialogue between the salesman and customer. This doesn't mean, however, that the customer wants to walk away, for this type of objection on the part of the customer is often just a challenge. If the challenge isn't met, and met correctly, then the sale is indeed terminated. Remember, this type of objection is sometimes thrown out because the customer wants to be convinced, and so these objections do offer you a chance to conclude a sale.

1. I'll think about it.
2. I can't make up my mind.
3. I'll come back some other time after I talk it over with my (friend, husband, wife, neighbor).
4. I don't have the time right now.
5. I'm not sure if my (wife, husband, friends) will like it.
6. I really didn't expect to buy it.
7. I'm just shopping around.
8. It's too big. I wouldn't know where to put it.
9. It's too small—I'm always losing things.
10. It's the wrong color (size, shape, appearance).
11. I don't want to have to wait so long for delivery.

ANALYZING OBJECTIONS

All the objections listed have many elements in common. People can all raise objections to price in different ways, but no matter how they do it, or how they state it, a price objection is just that.

ANTICIPATING OBJECTIONS

Some salesmen, realizing there will be some objections similar to those we have listed, do not prepare a sales pitch, but depend on their

Three Steps to a Sale

own native ability to handle the selling situation. Their reasoning is that they first want to listen to the customers, analyze their objections at home in a leisurely way, and then have the answers ready for the next customer. This sounds like a powerful and reasonable argument on the part of the salesman, but there are a number of things wrong with it.

1. The chances for *not* making a sale to the original customer (or customers) are good. Customers are not going to wait around while a salesman does his homework. They are not going to be patient and wait while the salesman learns how to be a salesman.

2. The salesman may not prepare his sales pitch because he is too lazy to do so. His arguments that he first wants to hear the customer's objections and then to analyze them at his leisure sound very much like rationalizations, that is, excuses for not doing his work.

3. A salesman who wants to wait for the day when he has enough selling experience to be able to prepare a perfect sales pitch will never prepare it for the simple reason there is no such thing as a perfect sales pitch.

The best way to be a salesman, a good salesman, is to make sales. You cannot be a good salesman without preparation.

But suppose your first effort at a sales pitch isn't a good one, what then? First, no one ever said that it would be good, just that it would be a start in the right direction. It would be most extraordinary if, as a beginning salesman, you started off with a perfect sales pitch. A good sales pitch is based on selling experience, but every sales pitch, no matter how good it is, is always started *before* selling, not during or after.

Therefore, for both types of objections—subjective and objective—the best assurance of a sale is adequate preparation. If you are starting in selling for the first time, here is what you should do:

1. Learn as much as you possibly can about the product or service

You Can Become A Super Salesman

you are expected to sell. Read the manufacturer's literature. Read any advertising placed by the manufacturer.

2. Examine the product. Use it. Touch it, feel it, take it apart. Find out what it can do and what it cannot do. Learn the price, the discount, the colors, shapes, and different sizes. Find out how the item is packaged, when it can be delivered, how it is shipped, and who pays the shipping charges. If there is more than one model of the item, learn the model numbers and the differences that exist between models. If the model has various operating controls, learn their names and what they are supposed to do. How much does it cost, if anything, to operate the item?

3. If you can, speak to other, more experienced salesman about the product. Don't be ashamed of being a novice salesman. Everyone has to start sometime. Salesmen are made, not born.

4. Learn as much as you can about competing products. Learn about the advantages your product has over other products. What weaknesses does it have? How does it compare pricewise?

After you have done all this (*before* actually selling), you will be well on your way toward completion of your sales pitch.

THE RISK OF AN ANSWER

The trouble with knowing the answers to questions you are sure will be asked is that you may be tempted to spill out a reply before the customer completes his question. This will give the customer the impression your answer is artificial or memorized. When you try to make a sale, you aren't in a race. Your answer must appear to be thought out. Note, though, that the competent, successful salesman does have answers. This doesn't mean that right at the start you will have the answer

Three Steps to a Sale

to all possible questions, but you will at least have the answers to most of them. If you can answer most questions, the customer will be satisfied. Under these circumstances, a simple, "I don't know, but I can find out for you" will satisfy most customers. But if you make a promise to find out, do so, as much for your own future sales pitch as for the present customer.

HOW TO HANDLE OBJECTIONS

There are two basic ways in which you can take care of a customer's objections.

THE HEAD-ON APPROACH

In this selling technique, you do not avoid the objection, but meet it squarely. Your customer may say something about your product that is not true, or he may attack the prestige of the company you represent, or he may make some caustic comments about your company and its line of products. The only way you can meet objections of this kind is with facts, clearly and politely stated. Remember, these objections are emotional in content and usually have no basis. You can overcome them with information you have previously acquired. Note, however, you cannot let objections of this kind go unchallenged. That is what we mean when we talk about the *head on approach*. The danger of letting such objections go unchallenged is that they always lose a sale. If a customer makes emotionally-loaded false assertions about the product you are selling or the company that makes it, and you do not meet the objection, the customer will properly assume his objections are true, and it is at this moment that the sale is lost.

You Can Become A Super Salesman

As an example, assume you have just heard a typical complaint: the product you are selling is of poor quality, or it is not as good as a competing product, or a friend has bought the product and is unhappy with it. These objections may be phrased in many different ways, but translated they all mean: the product isn't any good.

What can you say that will overcome such an objection?

Here is where your previously acquired product knowledge will come in handy.

1. The product has won three gold medals in international competition with competing products. The judges are all highly trained, impartial experts.

2. Our files are full of letters from satisfied customers who have nothing but praise for the product. I will be glad to let you go through our files, or I will bring the letters to you and show them to you.

3. Our products have been tested by an independent testing agency. Here is a copy of their report.

4. Our product has now been selling for years. We have thousands of satisfied customers.

5. Our company was established in (give year). They would long since have been out of business if their product was as bad as you claim it is.

6. Our product line is fully guaranteed. Our guaranty is for years.

7. We have service departments that will do any repairs, if they should ever be needed.

8. Yes, our product costs more, but we give you much more for the money.

These are just a few suggestions. Naturally, they may not all apply to the product you are about to sell, nor do we intend they should. Use them as a guide. The more of these answers you have on hand *before* selling, the greater your chance of concluding a sale. A customer's objection is a challenge, and if you fail to meet the challenge, the sale is lost.

Note the great difference between the objections and the answers. The objections are often based on emotion, personal habits of the customer, or his mental make-up. Your answers are *not* emotional; they are factual. A reply based on fact will nearly always demolish an objection based on emotion. But it will only do so if you have the information on hand before the objection is made.

THE UNANSWERABLE OBJECTION

It is always possible that your factual reply to the customer's emotional objections will not convince the customer. Not everyone is swayed by reason. You will always get some customers who will repeat their objections, even after you answer them. This simply indicates they are listening to themselves and not to you. You will then have a "no one can convince me" type of customer.

At this point it would be unwise to continue trying to meet the customer's objection. Tell your customer that you want to bypass this objection for the moment. Continue your sales pitch by talking about the quality of your product and its features. The reason for doing this is that the number of advantages may be so great they may completely overcome the single objection the customer has raised. If you can mention enough superior features of your product, you are more likely to sell it.

Also, remember there are always people looking for arguments, and they regard salespeople as fair game. Classify such people in the same category as those described earlier: people who use shopping as an entertainment device.

You Can Become A Super Salesman

WHAT'S NEXT?

The role of buyer and seller is an unusual one. For a short period of time, the buyer and seller are engaged in a close relationship. The salesman learns quite a bit about his prospective customer and quite often what he learns is ordinarily considered confidential information. He knows what the customer wants to buy, why he wants it, and how much he is ready to spend. He gets quite an insight into the customer's financial condition. On the other hand, the customer must take the salesman into his confidence. He must reveal information about himself that he normally regards as private.

In the next chapter you will learn more about salesman and buyer relationships, with additional information on how to meet customers' objections and more thoughts on how to build your sales pitch.

UNDERSTANDING WHAT YOU SELL

Some people not only have a false idea about salesmen, but also about the entire relationship between buyer and seller. It's easy enough to understand how it is possible for mistaken ideas to get started. In daily living, many products are sold by clerks. The customer selects the item, possibly from a counter, and hands it to the clerk, together with the money to pay for the product. There is no selling involved here. The clerk is not a salesman or saleswoman but a clerk, an order taker. The customer assumes two roles: that of the customer and that of the salesperson. In effect, the customer sells himself (or herself) the product. There are no objections, no discussions.

Because this type of purchase is made so often, it is logical to think that if a person needs something, all he must do is go out and buy it. It isn't quite that easy for a number of reasons. First, people aren't simple, rather they are complex. People will often not buy, even though they may need a particular product. They want to be sold. They want to be convinced. They want to learn more about the product. They want to be reassured.

Second, many people enjoy the position of buyer. It gives them a feeling of power, the ability to control the income, hence the living conditions, of another person. It makes them feel looked up to and respected. They occupy the center of stage. For a time, however short, they are the "boss" and others do what they say. Finally, the buyer may be motivated by any combination of these factors. The buyer can be quite a complex individual.

THE BORDERLINE BUYER

There are some people who will never buy unless a salesman is present. They will not go into a store, make their own selection, and then ask to have it wrapped. They want to be waited upon. They want to discuss their purchase, preferably with someone who presumably knows quite a bit about the product, that is, the salesman. They want personal service. This type of buyer may not mention price but will wait for the salesman to bring up the subject. For buyers of this kind, price is generally not a valid objection.

THE JOY OF THE JOB

By now you can appreciate that you will meet a wide variety of people, ranging from those who will bargain over the cost of an item down to the last penny, to those who couldn't care less about price, but insist on the personal services of a salesman. In between these two

You Can Become A Super Salesman

extremes you will find all sorts of people. For the true salesman or saleswoman this provides job interest they could not possibly find in any other occupation. To the salesman, meeting people is a continual challenge and is also a source of pleasure (whether he admits it or not). But this is true only if the salesman is prepared, that is, if he is confident of being able to meet objections and knows his product thoroughly. Note the great advantage the salesman has. He is prepared; the customer is not. He knows the product; the customer does not. He is thoroughly familiar with the various kinds of objections the customer can make and knows all the answers; the customer does not. The experienced and prepared salesman likes the challenge of a new sale because he is prepared. The customer is not.

Unlike other kinds of jobs, the chance to meet new people creates a kind of excitement. Selling is never the same, and so never becomes like other jobs—the same work, day after day.

ONCE AGAIN—YOUR SALES PITCH

A sales pitch is composed of two basic factors: information and answers to objections. In your sales pitch you must tell your prospective customer about the product. What you are doing is supplying information the prospect is unwilling or unable to get for himself. The prospect may have had his curiosity aroused by an ad, or he may have heard about your product from a friend, or he may have seen it somewhere. His first motivation is the need for more information, therefore, supplying information is an important part of any sales pitch. In a sense, then, you are a teacher, but be careful. You are not in a classroom and the customer isn't a captive pupil who cannot walk out. A customer can and will walk away if you talk down to him, if you give him the impression he is

Understanding What You Sell

ignorant and you are smart, or if he gets the idea you feel superior to him because you know about the product and he does not. If you talk down to your prospect, he will soon recognize it and will resent it. Don't be patronizing.

Don't force your customer to dig for information. Some salesmen have the habit of supplying information almost grudgingly. If the customer has to pull information out of you, he will soon build a sales resistance that will surprise you.

The opposite extreme, of course, is the salesman who floods the prospect with information that is neither requested nor wanted. If, for example, a customer wants to know about color, explain the various colors available, those colors regarded as most popular, the most durable colors, the most practical colors. Don't go off on a tangent about size, shape, or style.

THE "ACCORDION" SALES PITCH

The process of revising your sales pitch often means adding information to it, generally in the form of answering a customer's objections. Since most of your sales pitch is made up of two parts—product information and answers to objections—you won't need to make too many changes in product information if you've done the job right the first time. The only time you will need to make such changes is when the manufacturer of your product brings out a revised model or brings out new models. You will always keep adding to your store of "objection answers," however, because as you get more and more involved in selling, you will keep coming across new objections. Eventually, you will find you have quite an elaborate and lengthy sales pitch.

Does this mean you must give every customer the same sales

approach? Definitely not. Some customers will be partially pre-sold through exposure to advertising or discussions with friends or neighbors. They may have very little need for information, and they may have very few objections. If you insist on going through your entire sales pitch, you will only see these prospective customers disappear.

On the other hand, you may have prospects who have never heard of your product, know nothing about it, and have a lengthy mental list of questions and objections. For such customers you must be prepared to have a lengthy sales pitch. That is why we refer to the sales pitch as an accordion. It must be longer or shorter, depending on the demand.

EDUCATING THE CUSTOMER

At one extreme you will have a customer who knows absolutely nothing about the product you are selling, but who has indicated some interest in it. At the other extreme you will have the customer who probably knows almost as much about the product as you do. Fortunately, both of these extremes represent a minority, for they can be troublesome. Most customers come somewhere in between these two.

THE FEARFUL CUSTOMER

The customer who knows absolutely nothing about your product, but has developed an interest in it, may be fearful. He is attracted, but repelled. He wants the product, but because it is so new, or so different, is afraid. This means your pitch must emphasize the educational aspect. As the prospective customer learns more and more about the product, some of his fears will begin to disappear. And, because you are the one who

Understanding What You Sell

removed his fears, he will have confidence in you. This becomes an excellent basis for making a sale.

THE "KNOW-IT-ALL" CUSTOMER

Since we are still talking about extremes, consider the customer who thinks he knows more about the product than you do. Somehow, through reading or experience, or both, he has acquired a broad background of knowledge. For a customer of this type, then, what is needed is not education, but a sales pitch that will emphasize answers to objections.

STEPS TO MORE SALES

To become an effective salesman, then, here is what you must do:

First, make up a sales presentation or sales pitch. For those who are first starting in selling, it is a good idea to write out all ideas. Start by writing as much as you know about the product. List these ideas as 1, 2, 3, and so forth. Try to make the list as complete as possible.

Second, write all the possible objections to your product followed by your answers.

Third, after you have made this list, you will have a large part of your sales pitch. Keep the list and add to it as you gain selling experience. At the beginning, read the list daily until you know it thoroughly. In time, you will know it by memory and so the list, your sales pitch, will become a mental record, rather than written.

How will you know when your sales pitch must be modified? When

You Can Become A Super Salesman

a customer asks a question you cannot answer. When you learn something about the product you did not know before.

THE DEMONSTRATION

Some products require a demonstration for a sale; others do not. If you are selling cosmetics, you may let a customer sniff a bottle of perfume. If you are selling vacuum cleaners you may have a demonstration model out on a floor showing how the cleaner is used. If you are selling cars, you may let the customer sit in the car, or let him take a test drive. Not all products can be demonstrated. If you are selling books, there is nothing to demonstrate. If you are selling liquor, there is nothing to demonstrate.

If the product you are selling does require a demonstration or if a demonstration will help you conclude a sale, then you must be thoroughly familiar with the product. If you start looking for the different controls, if you are unable to make the product work as it should, if you are unable to demonstrate that the product will do everything you claim it can do, then there will be no sale. Actually, you should be able to demonstrate the product blindfolded.

During the time you are making a demonstration, you can continue your sales pitch. At this time call the customer's attention to the ease of handling the controls, to the convenience of the unit, to the good job it is doing, to its attractive appearance. Also, watch your customer's reactions, and answer any possible objections. Determine in your own mind just how long you will continue the demonstration before attempting to close the sale. If you know your sales pitch and you know the product, then the demonstration will be surrounded by an air of sureness and confidence.

Understanding What You Sell

DEMONSTRATIONS AND COMPARISONS

What if the product you are selling isn't the kind you can demonstrate? This doesn't mean you shouldn't become familiar with it. Assume it is an item that is sold in some sort of box or bottle. Hold the box or bottle in your hands so you will know just how it feels to the customer. Read every word on the front label, then read every word on the back label. Don't let yourself get caught by a customer who likes to read the fine print. A few very valid objections may be lurking somewhere in the statements on the labels. Be prepared to meet them.

SERVICE SALES

In selling a service, you will be selling an idea or a concept, hence there will be nothing for you to demonstrate. Since this kind of selling does require considerable experience there's not much point in discussing it in detail. We should tell you, however, that this kind of selling requires extensive preparation. Such salesmen often come equipped with charts, tables, graphs, and other pictorial presentations to put across their selling points.

HOW TO HANDLE COMPETITION

We live in a competitive society, and while you may think it would be pleasant to have no competition, you should be realistic enough to be able to meet those people who are working against you for their share of the sales dollar. There are two types of competition: from salesmen selling the same product you do and from salesmen pushing competing items.

As far as competing with other salesmen selling what you are selling is concerned, all you can do is try to be a better salesman. This isn't as difficult as it sounds. They are human, have their lazy moments, discouraging days, and low sales record days. Do the best you know how, and then try just a little bit harder.

To meet the threat of competing products you should know their various features, but do not mention competing products when you are making a sale. Discuss them only if your customer refers to them as an objection. If your customer does bring up the subject, however, you can then be in the advantageous position of comparing the item you are selling (with all its benefits) against the disadvantages of the competing product. This may be especially necessary if the competing item is cheaper than the product you are selling.

As an example, suppose you are an electrical appliances salesman and your prospective customer has just told you she can buy a competing item for less money. What can you do about it? Here is a list of suggestions:

1. Your product may cost a little more, but isn't it generally true that we get what we pay for? Your product is higher in price but its quality is much greater. Your product has a longer life, a longer guarantee, and will not rust or wear out as quickly.

2. Because your product is so much better, it will require less servicing or repair, so, in the long run, your product actually costs less.

3. Your product is more economical to operate. Over a period of time it will actually pay for itself.

4. Your product is easier to use; the controls are simpler and anyone can operate them.

Understanding What You Sell

5. Your product is safer. The wiring has been checked and double-checked. Every part is subjected to mechanical and electrical inspection.
6. Your product carries a longer warranty.
7. The company making your product has been in business longer, is better known, is more highly advertised. Its products are used by more people.
8. Yes, your product does cost a bit more, but quality construction and quality materials always cost more.
9. You will be able to speak with pride to your neighbors and friends about this product. Since it isn't a cheap item (a reference to the competing product), it isn't anything to be ashamed of.
10. The best is cheapest in the long run.
11. Your product is more durable.
12. The product is nationally advertised on TV, radio, and in magazines.

Of course it may not be necessary to use all these answers to overcome just one objection. It all depends on the customer and the product. If the customer isn't making a strenuous objection about price, then just one or two statements will do. If the customer seems quite upset about the higher price of the product you are selling, you may have to supply more answers.

ADD TO THE LIST

This list of possible answers to an objection about a lower-priced competing item isn't complete, but should give you an idea of what to say. You can see that what is involved here is a thorough knowledge of what you are selling *plus* a knowledge of what your competition is up to.

You Can Become A Super Salesman

What are we asking you to do? We are asking you to know your job, but this is true of any job. You wouldn't go to a physician who had no confidence in his own ability. You wouldn't hire a plumber who seemed bewildered by his tools. You wouldn't get into a taxi being driven by someone who was obviously inexperienced. Yet, there are some people who have the strange notion that there is nothing to selling, but selling, like any other profession, requires preparation. The more you prepare, the more you study and analyze your own product line and the product line of your competition, the greater chance you have for success.

THE EDUCATED CUSTOMER

Because of the growth of newspapers, magazines, radio, and TV, today's customer is far more knowledgeable than those of a decade or so ago. Quite often, the customer knows what he wants and what he expects before he confronts a salesman. The average consumer today is far more alert and more difficult to persuade. In addition, there is no shortage of highly advertised competing products. For these reasons, you will encounter more and more customers who have a "show me" attitude.

Now you can see the importance of knowing your product and the need for a smooth, easily handled demonstration. This is a byproduct of the customer's "show me" attitude. You can also understand that a good salesman of some ten years ago or more may not be as good a salesman if he has failed to update his approach. What is true of yesterday may not be true of tomorrow. You cannot assume that a perfectly operating sales pitch you managed to develop for today's use will be as valid a year or two from today.

There is one thing you can say with assurance about customers —they will change.

Understanding What You Sell

BACK TO THE DEMONSTRATION

If you can make a demonstration, it will be an important part of your sales pitch. A demonstration is also of value because you can make it to a number of possible customers at the same time, and therefore you have an opportunity of producing volume sales, rather than single sales.

There are all kinds of demonstrations. Some are made in department stores; others are made in the home. Some are given at fairs, shows, conventions, or meetings. Sometimes a salesman will arrange to give a demonstration to a number of his prospects at the same time and may arrange for the demonstration in the office or showroom of a manufacturer.

Before telling you more about what a demonstration is, let us start by telling you what it is not. It is not a lecture. It is not an exercise in which you hear the sound of your own voice. It is not a professor talking to his students. It is not a smart person talking to a group of stupid people. It is not someone who is gracious and kind enough to condescend talking to a group.

Now you may find it incredible that there are salesmen with such obviously wrong attitudes, but there are. The next time you have an opportunity to watch a salesman in action giving a demonstration, do so. You will be impressed by some salesmen, but many of them will leave you with the thought of "how did they ever become salesmen?"

FEATURES OF A GOOD DEMONSTRATION

Now let's move along to the positive side and see, point by point, the main features of a good demonstration.

First, start by reviewing the features most likely to interest the

You Can Become A Super Salesman

prospective customer (or customers). How do you know which features the customer is really interested in? You will know if you were listening to the customer's opening comments. He (or she or they) may have said something about the price (a common type of opening statement), size, style, or shape. There may have been a question about delivery time. The customer may even have started with a disparaging statement comparing your product unfavorably with some competitor's product.

But whatever the customer said, that is your starting point because that is what the customer is interested in at this moment. If the prospect starts with a challenge about the price, you can talk for a week about color, size and delivery, but he will not be interested until you resolve the thing foremost in his mind—the price.

Second, assuming your customer started by mentioning price, should you simply state the price and then continue along other lines? No. Watch the customer's reaction. If the customer accepts the price calmly, without challenge, without interrupting to say something about it, you can move right along to some other part of your sales pitch. You haven't received an objection.

If, however, the customer seems disturbed or resentful or annoyed, or hostile, or angry, or dissatisfied, you have been given a clue as to where to begin your demonstration. You start with price. While showing the product and demonstrating its many desirable features you emphasize:

1. The price seems high but represents a long time economy.
2. The superior quality of the product means a modest price increase over competing lines.
3. There is no such thing as a cheap product; only products cheaply made. A less expensive item than the one you are selling means more money spent in upkeep, in repairs, and so on.

Third, once you have overcome the price objection, continue the demonstration with those characteristics of your product that can be seen

Understanding What You Sell

immediately: color, size, style, overall appearance, and attractiveness. It is true the customer is looking at the product but this doesn't mean he really sees it. If the product has some special features, call attention to them.

But why should you tell a customer about something he can see for himself? Why bother showing something and talking about something that is right there under the customer's eyes. The reason is based on an understanding of human nature. If you tell your customer about something he can verify, you establish your own credibility. The customer can see for himself, at once, you are telling the truth. At the start, the customer doesn't know you and has no reason to trust you. On the contrary, the customer may really be suspicious and wait for you to make a false statement or some statement that he can challenge. If you talk about the obvious features of your product, he can immediately verify them and his attitude of suspicion can be changed to one of acceptance. It sounds elementary, but that's the way it is. Remember, it isn't your job to change human nature, but to bend it to your advantage. You cannot get good sales or consistent sales by being bitter or disillusioned about the way customers react. They react the way they do because they are human beings. Don't try to fight human nature, instead, work with it and you will be a better and more successful salesman.

Fourth, go from the easily understandable and obvious facets of the product to those that aren't so easy to understand and aren't apparent to the customer. If your audience is non-technical, don't use technical language. Be careful you do not lose your audience, that is, don't talk about your product in terms they do not understand or that they are unable to follow. Watch their faces. If they look as though they do not understand, stop. It is more important for you to get your message across rather than to complete your sales pitch.

Fifth, encourage your customer to ask questions while you are

You Can Become A Super Salesman

demonstrating. The more questions that are asked, the closer you are to a sale. You may wonder, "aren't a customer's questions a nuisance when you are making a sales pitch?" They are if you don't want to be a salesman. You should regard a customer's questions as a sign of progress. The worst kind of customer is one who will let you go through your entire sales pitch without saying a single word or raising a single objection. He is the customer who will probably just walk away. The fact that a customer does ask questions is a sign of interest. It is an indication you can sell your product.

Sixth, get your customer (or customers) involved in the demonstration. It is a fact that a sale is easier to make when the customer takes part in the demonstration and is thus able to prove for himself that the salesman's statements are true. Another reason for involving your customer in the demonstration is called a "sense of ownership." This means that when you allow a customer to use a product, the customer visualizes himself as the owner. What happens then is that the customer takes on a dual role: that of salesman and prospect. The customer is now in the position of selling himself. There are customers who come into a store, select some item, and pay for it without a word of conversation passing between themselves and the clerk behind a counter. When a customer takes part in a demonstration, it becomes similar to the customer buying without a salesman.

A good example of this is the way in which car salesmen sell automobiles. One of the first things they do during a presentation is to invite the prospect to sit in the car—to get behind the wheel. They do this even though the car is in a showroom with no possibility of getting the car into motion. Physical contact between a sales prospect and the product is important in making a sale. In certain types of sales this is an essential part of the entire relationship between customer and salesman. In the case of furs, clothing, shoes, hats, jewelry, contact between the customer and

Understanding What You Sell

the product is part of the sale. The opening sentence of salesmen in clothing stores is, for example: "Here. I know this suit isn't the color you asked for, but let's try it on for size." The salesman may know the customer's size. The customer probably has mentioned it. That has nothing to do with it. The salesman knows that if he wants to make a sale, the customer must make prompt contact with the product. It is important for the customer to visualize himself as the owner of a new suit.

There is still another reason for customer participation. You are, in effect, proving your own faith in the product. You are establishing the fact that this is the kind of product you want to sell. You are telling the customer: "Don't take my word for it. Try it for yourself and you will see I mean every word I say."

COMPARISON SHOPPERS

Sooner or later, and generally sooner, you will have customers who are comparison shoppers. These customers will not buy until they have thoroughly covered the product field. The fact is they may often spend more time and money in comparison shopping than the savings they may make. People of this kind enjoy shopping. They like talking to salesmen. You will find they take a great interest in products, ask many questions, raise few objections. As a group they know fairly well what they want, and they also have a good idea about price. They recognize bargains when they see them. At the same time, they are also quick to recognize overpriced items. They are quality conscious and do not object to paying more money, provided they receive quality at what they consider a good price.

It isn't always easy to change a comparison shopper to a buyer, but keep this in mind. Sooner or later the comparison shopper must settle

You Can Become A Super Salesman

down and make a purchase. The best way to handle this type of shopper is to know the competing product or products. You may not be in a position, however, to evaluate competing lines as thoroughly as you would like. You may not have either the time or the opportunity, but there are ways of overcoming this. You can get printed literature describing competing items. You can arrange to have yourself put on the mailing lists of your competitors, for such lists are seldom checked thoroughly. You can also learn more about your competition by reading their ads in consumer or trade magazines, or by listening to their ads on radio and television.

Also, speak to other salesmen about competing products, and try to learn from them the strengths and the weaknesses of such products. Perhaps your neighbors or your friends have purchased such items. If they have, talk to them, or try to get them to let you use the products. You can learn a lot about your competition by having some "on hand" experience. Find out for yourself if people who have bought competing products are satisfied. Does the product really live up to the salesman's statements? Would they buy the same product again?

There is one thing you should *not* do and that is to consider a competitor's products as inferior simply because they are sold by a competitor. This isn't a question of emotion, but of fact. You cannot shrug off your competitor's claims without knowing something about the product, and the only way to know is to learn. Then, when the subject of competing products is brought up by comparison shoppers—or by any other kind of shopper—you will be in a position to refute statements with facts based on your own research, reading, studying, questioning, and listening.

If you have the time, assume the role of a customer and let the competing salesman try his sales pitch on you. Also, if you have the time, do some comparison shopping. Visit stores that carry the competing line and see if you can learn more about it. Naturally, you will never know a

Understanding What You Sell

competing line as well as you do your own, but you shouldn't ever use this as an excuse.

There are many ways of learning about other products, and if you follow through on this aggressively, you will acquire enough information and knowledge to be able to answer any customer's questions completely.

There is one thing you should know. You may be sure that the product you are selling has been purchased by the competitor (or competitors), that it has been analyzed, measured, weighed, taken apart, put together, checked, tested and discussed. Some product manufacturers do this for their own benefit to see how they compare with others, or to see if they can get some new ideas about manufacturing or design, or to learn more about what their competitor is doing. Quite often this information is kept secret, but some manufacturers pass the results of their investigations along to their salesmen. It is a wise company that does so.

SHOULD YOU ENGAGE IN COMPARISONS?

Some salesmen do make an in-depth study of competing products, and then, to show they have done their homework, deliberately bring up the subject of other products during their sales pitch.

Don't do it!

The only time you should make comparisons is if the customer brings up the subject and opens the door to this approach. As far as you are concerned, a competing product doesn't even exist during your sales pitch. To discuss it on your own initiative is to add a distracting element to your sales presentation. Some salesmen do this as a matter of routine. They may do it to "show off," or to indicate how well they know the entire market, or to try to impress the customer. However, it is poor selling and is often self-defeating.

CONTROLLING THE SALE

Try not to let any discussion with your customer get out of your control. You will always have customers who are time wasters and who will look for opportunities to get you to talk with them about anything except the product. They will try to steer the discussion, that is, your sales pitch, into a dozen other directions, including the weather, local sports, or politics. Selling is not a social gathering. Yes, some sales are made on golf courses or over a game of bridge or in a bar, but this is a limited, highly specialized form of selling. Always keep your goal in mind—to keep your product the center of the discussion. You shouldn't spend more than a minute or two to talk about anything else but the product.

KNOCKING THE COMPETITION

You may be strongly tempted but you should not, under any circumstances, poke fun at, make jokes of, or "knock" a competing product. You never know, it could be the product you may be selling some day. If your customer does bring up the subject of a competing product, then, and only then, you need do two things:
1. Emphasize the fact that so many people are using your product.
2. Admit that the competing product is good, but yours is superior in many respects.

Understanding What You Sell

Many people have a distrust of someone who downgrades a competing product. They will suspect you of trying to make a sale by stepping on someone else. Further, many people have an instinctive sympathy for the underdog, and all you may be doing when downtalking a competitor is arousing this sympathy. At the same time you will be encouraging a feeling of hostility that will be directed toward you and also toward the product you are selling.

MENTIONING THE COMPETITION

We would suggest you follow the guidance of one noted American salesman who said: "It is acceptable to talk about competition in your discussion, but if you do, you should refer to the matter in general terms, without specific references about one particular competitor."

What does this mean? First, never mention the name of a competitor to a customer. The customer may do so, but you should not. Second, if you make a comparison, do so between related products. If the customer brings up the subject of comparison prices, stick to the subject of comparison prices. If the customer brings up the subject of a particular feature a competing product has, discuss this feature specifically, and when you do, don't be vague or general. Answer the question or objection in a definite manner, and then move ahead with your sales pitch. It may be that your product has one or two qualities that are inferior to the competition. So what? There is no single product made which is superior in every respect. The point is to emphasize all of the superior characteristics of your product.

You Can Become A Super Salesman

WORDS THAT MAKE SALES

There are certain words in selling called *trigger* words because they produce definite reactions on the part of your prospect. First, there are certain words you should avoid. Don't use words such as "superior" or "better" in describing the item you are selling. If it were not a superior or better product you wouldn't be selling it, and so in using these words you may give the impression you aren't quite sure yourself. Act as though your product is completely the best in every respect.

There are words and phrases that will impress the customer. These are "different taste" or "different style" or "different type." Words such as "new," "latest," "just released," "most technically advanced," are helpful. Other words such as "convenient to use," "time saver," "money saver," "economical in operation," should be part of your pitch.

Examine the ads in your local newspaper and you will see that many of them emphasize savings. You will find phrases such as "save more than 20 percent" or "now reduced" or "if you buy now, you will save." You can learn quite a bit about words you should use by reading such ads, particularly their headlines. The reason for this is that customers do not like to be reminded they are spending money. It sounds contrary, but what the customer likes to think is not that he is spending, but saving. Therefore, a sales pitch must include a word, preferably a number of words, to the effect that the purchase will mean savings, or the product will pay for itself, or that the price has been reduced by   percent, or that the customer will save in the long run by buying the product now. This savings concept can also be used if your product is higher priced than the competition. Yours is a better product, and although it does cost a bit more, it will result in greater savings. Note that the higher cost is played down. No matter how much more your product does cost, it "only costs a bit more." Remember, savings are always emphasized. Many salesmen and advertisers like to use percentages, "will save you 30 percent or more," and so forth.

Here are some other time-tested phrases:

Lasts longer

Wears better

Modern styling

Easy to use

Next to the savings concept, the "convenience" feature is of great importance. Does the product you are selling have any convenience features, especially features competing products do not have? Does it have a foot pedal, so the customer doesn't have to bend over. Perhaps it shuts itself off. Maybe it has controls that simplify operation of the product. Is it more convenient to store? Does it have parts that come out or go in automatically? Whatever the convenience features are, emphasize them.

THE DETAILS OF SALESMANSHIP

Successful salesmanship is based on attention to many small details. As you acquire experience in selling you will soon be alert to the things most people do not notice. You will know more about people. You will soon be able to tell, just from the expression on a customer's face, or his use of a few words, what he is looking for, how much he expects to spend, and how quickly you can close the sale. A well-known and highly successful real-estate salesman once claimed he could tell just how much his prospects wanted to spend for a house within one or two minutes after talking to them. His sales record proved his claim.

But aren't there some eccentric buyers, that is, buyers who are extremely wealthy, who dress in a very poor way, and who always manage to deceive salesmen? Yes, in the movies. In real life people who have money to spend dress and buy accordingly. When you have a chance to meet a prospective buyer, take a good look, not just a casual one. What sort of appearance does the buyer have? Is he well-dressed, poorly dressed? What sort of words does the customer use? Is he well-spoken, poorly educated, well-educated? If a husband and wife are both involved in making the purchase, which is the dominant one? Which one will sign a check or make payment? At a recent hotel convention, attended by husbands and wives, out of 20 people waiting in line to check out and pay for their rooms, 19 were women and they paid by check. The man of the house isn't always the treasurer. When selling a single product to two people at the same time, you should look and listen to decide which one will actually make the purchase. If a man takes his wife along when he buys a suit it could very well be the wife who will make the buying decision. No matter how well your sales pitch works on the man, it will be ineffective if it does not reach the woman. The same thinking also applies if two girls are together, or two men. One of the two will always be the decision maker, and it is that one who must be sold. The other will go along.

SALESMEN AND ORDER TAKERS

There are two types of salesmen, although both groups should not be classified as such. The first group consists of true salesmen. These are the men and women to whom selling is a profession. They are constantly trying to improve their selling techniques. They are always adding to their personal store of selling knowledge. They generally work on a commission, bonus, or override basis, even though some of them may also get a fixed salary. You will find them entering every selling contest open to them. You will find them studying their product line. They always try to evaluate their customers. They do their best to supply their customers with good service. They keep their selling promises. They try to build a loyal following of customers. In short, they do not regard the sale as the end of a relationship, but the beginning. They take pride in their selling ability.

The other group consists of order takers. The young lady or young man behind a counter who is handed an item plus cash from a customer isn't a salesman, but an order taker. They have no sales pitch and wouldn't know what you meant if you called it to their attention. They do not care whether the customer buys or not. They know little or nothing about the products they handle. All they do, as far as selling is concerned, is to hand across something the customer wants to buy. You've seen them. You'll find at least one, and generally more, in any department store. Quite often, to the order taker, the customer is a nuisance. The order taker will sometimes make the customer wait, either deliberately or through laziness. A salesman never does this.

Can an order taker ever become a salesman? Yes, if the order taker is ambitious, wants to earn more, wants to get ahead in life, and is dissatisfied with his job. While the order taker thinks he has security, because he gets a weekly salary, that security isn't on as sound a basis as you might think. His salary is usually low and he can be easily replaced because there are thousands just like him. The job of the order taker can be dull, for although he may face hundreds of people every day, there is no contact. His customers are a blur of faces. There is no dialogue. He does not really meet people. The world of the buyer and that of the seller are clearly separated.

Can a salesman ever become an order taker? Yes, it does happen. It sometimes takes place when a salesman develops a limited number of

You Can Become A Super Salesman

customers, knows all their buying habits, knows just what they want, and also knows his own product line thoroughly. The salesman has settled down into a routine in which he will have no more challenges, will make no more money. He is on a somewhat higher level than the clerk behind the counter in a store, but not that much. He may travel, but his route is always the same. He does see customers, but they are always the same. He may rarely use his sales pitch, but never revises or updates it because he does not want to do so. There is a ceiling on his income, but he is the one who fixed it at that position. He is not interested in special promotions, special sales, nor does he make any effort to earn additional commissions or bonuses.

THE NEED FOR KNOWING YOUR PRODUCT

A thorough product knowledge is not only important in making a sales demonstration, but it also enables you to emphasize certain points.

1. You will know how to highlight your product's benefits clearly and convincingly. In time you will learn which of these benefits sound most attractive to the potential buyer.
2. If your company brings out a new model, your knowledge of earlier products will enable you to make valuable comparisons. You will look for new features, new selling points, and you will add these to your store of selling knowledge.
3. Keep in mind that one sale may lead to additional sales. Your product may be the type that lends itself to repeat orders. If you have a following of satisfied customers, you will find repeat sales not only financially satisfying, but much easier to do than the first sale. But what if your product isn't a repeat item? What if the sale is a "single item"? A good impression on a customer—a

Understanding What You Sell

satisfied customer—can lead to "word-of-mouth" recommendations.

4. If you know your product, you will be able to answer all of your customer's questions accurately and with confidence. This confidence will show itself in your selling behavior. In a customer-buyer relationship, salesmanship confidence is contagious. If you are confident because you know your product, your customer will soon notice it and will be affected by it. But if you aren't interested enough in your product to know all about it, why should your prospective customer be more interested?

5. Product knowledge builds customer respect. If you know your product your customer will look on you as an authority and will respect you for it.

WHAT'S NEXT?

Up to now the emphasis has been on two factors: the need for studying and evaluating your customer, and the need for being thoroughly familiar with the product or products you are selling. But there is still another factor you should know about, and that is yourself. How well do you know yourself? What characteristics do you have that should be emphasized to make you into a top-notch salesman? What part of your individuality should you suppress to improve your selling ability?

Selling is a close relationship between buyer and seller. How do you fit into that relationship? What can you do to improve it?

FOR SUCCESSFUL SELLING— UNDERSTAND YOURSELF

What is a salesman?

Is he something special, something different, something unique? First, here is what a salesman is not. He is not a machine or an orator. A salesman isn't someone who has more words at his command than anyone else. A salesman isn't someone who has the "gift of gab."

A salesman is just a human being with all of the human emotions of the rest of us—all of the fears, worries, anxieties, doubts, and problems. There is one big difference, though. A good salesman is aware that just as he reacts to his customers, so do his customers react to him. Salesmen are people, too. There are cranky customers; there are cranky salesmen. There are lazy customers; there are lazy salesmen.

THE SELLING PERSONALITY

Why should you be interested in being told that salesmen have typically human emotions? The important factor here is that many sales involve a face-to-face relationship with people. There are some forms of selling, however, in which the salesman never meets his customers. But there is also a large group of salesmen who make a living by meeting people and selling these people some product or service.

THE PERSONAL CONFRONTATION

When a salesman does meet his customers, there is a discussion between them, and it is this face-to-face meeting that can mean a successful sale or a failure. But there are so many different kinds of people. How can a salesman adapt to each one? How can a salesman recognize the many different types and adjust his selling approach accordingly?

SELF-CONTROL

Probably the most important adjustment any individual must make to become a successful salesman or saleswoman is to learn self-control. The customer often operates on an emotional basis; the salesman cannot afford the luxury of emotional behavior. The salesman can appeal to a customer's emotions, but he should not become involved in them.

If a salesman has a reaction to a customer that contains aggression, hostility, or impertinence, the potential sale is endangered. This has nothing to do with the quality or the value of the product. The customer may want the product, may be convinced of its value, and yet will buy a competing product simply because he has been alienated by a salesman.

CUSTOMER TYPES

The majority of customers are reasonable, pleasant to work with people, and can be convinced by the correct sales pitch. But included among them you will find:

1. The customer who is an out-and-out liar.
2. The provocative customer—the one who is looking for an argument or fight.
3. The resentful customer—the customer who always resents buying.
4. The phony—the customer who plays an artificial role, who may be out to defraud the salesman.
5. The emotional customer—the customer who is always in the grip of some kind of mood, such as intense elation or deep depression.
6. The customer with problems—the customer who is looking for a sympathetic ear and who thinks the salesman should supply it.

Although only six types of customers are listed here, there are more. Furthermore, they aren't always distinctive, that is, you may face a customer who is pleasant in every other respect, but does have a substantial amount of worries and fears that come to the surface when a sale is in progress.

For Successful Selling—Understand Yourself

SELF-HELP STEPS FOR A SALESMAN

What can a salesman do? What should he do? The first step is to exercise control. Like all of us, the salesman has problems, but unlike many of us, the salesman must learn to leave his problems at home. If he cannot do that, then he must learn to control himself. There is no doubt that some customers would try the patience of a saint. There is also no doubt that some customers can and do release their hostilities on the first available victim—often a salesman. Remember also that the realtionship of buyer and seller means the buyer has the power in his hands; the buyer is in a position to make the decision to buy or not to buy. Some people become intoxicated with this sense of power, enjoy it, try to dramatize it, and drag it out as long as possible. Some people enjoy the customer-salesman relationship because they regard it as putting them in a superior position, and in a certain sense it does. But if the salesman is a good judge of human nature, and he must learn to be if he is to be successful, then he will immediately evaluate the personality of his customer and will act accordingly.

A salesman must make his own personality flexible. He cannot be rigid and unbending. If a customer makes a false statement about the product being sold, if the statement is an out and out lie, the salesman can only react with facts, not emotion. It is quite natural to respond emotionally; it is unsalesmanlike.

A SALESMAN'S REACTIONS

What determines a salesman's reactions?

The answer to this question is in the salesman's own characteristics, as reflected in his own personality. Does this mean, then, you must try to change your personality to become a successful salesman? No, it doesn't mean that at all. It does mean that if you want to become truly successful, you must master your own personality characteristics. If one of the characteristics of your personality is a strong temper, go ahead and lose it. A temper can still be a big part of your own individual personality but don't let your temper control you or your job or your sales volume. Select the time and the place, but make sure both of them are at a time and place far removed from the selling area.

A salesman probably suffers more from frustration than any other professional. A salesman may do his homework, prepare an excellent sales pitch, have a product that brings out his enthusiasm, but may lose one sale after another. We all have bad days, but the customer must not become the victim of the salesman's frustrations. There are some companies in Japan that have rooms set aside with large rag-stuffed human-like figures that can be punched endlessly by tension-filled employees. A salesman may not have this opportunity, but there is no reason why a salesman cannot relieve his tensions through aggressive bowling, tennis, boxing, or some other sport. The only requirement for the salesman is that he must postpone his frustrations until some later, more appropriate time and place.

No, no one will ever claim that this is an easy thing to do, but it is essential.

WHAT IS THE FIRST STEP?

Before you can change yourself or before you can guide your personality into a more desirable selling form, you must be aware of the

For Successful Selling—Understand Yourself

need for a change. You cannot change unless you know that a change is necessary. In other words, a successful salesman understands himself. He knows his personality characteristics, he knows which of these characteristics act as a block in selling and he faces up to them. It isn't easy. It is much less difficult to imagine you have a personality that should not be modified. But you can put your feet right on the road to successful selling if you know your weaknesses and resolve to do something about them.

Quite often, the only thing that may stand between a salesman and a successful selling career is the personality of the salesman. It is true that a good salesman has faith in his product and also has a positive belief in his own ability to sell that product, but those important qualities are not enough. A salesman who manages to irritate his customers might find it difficult to give his product away, let alone to sell it.

SELLING YOURSELF

What is the job of a salesman?

One answer might be that a salesman's job is to sell a product or a service. This answer is only partially correct. A good salesman must often sell himself. Exactly what do we mean by this? A good salesman deliberately tries to build his own personality so that to the customer the personal relationship is the foundation on which the sale—and possibly repeat sales—is made. This doesn't mean the customer will readily buy shoddy, overpriced materials. It does mean that if a product has quality, if it is competitively priced, the salesman with the more desirable personality will get the order.

You Can Become A Super Salesman

WHAT IS A DESIRABLE PERSONALITY?

What is a desirable personality? Does it mean that a salesman must become a yes man catering to the customer's every whim and wish? Does it mean a salesman must be a happy personality, a life-of-the-party type, ever ready with a joke, and constantly wearing a smile? Hardly, for this kind of personality would be as obnoxious as the type who shows his personal problems in his face. There are, however, certain personality characteristics a salesman should have and should especially have for building a repeat-sale type of business.

IMAGINE YOU ARE THE CUSTOMER

Put yourself in the customer's place.

Wouldn't you rather do business with a salesman on whom you could depend? In other words, a desirable personality characteristic of a salesman is reliability. If a salesman quotes a price, you certainly don't want to have any doubts that this is the price you will pay. And if a salesman supplies a delivery date, you want to be able to depend on that date. If a salesman tells you the product is guaranteed for a specific amount of time, you want to be able to depend on that guarantee.

But what about all of these qualities? Don't they hinge on just a single word—reliability.

Reliability is sometimes known by other names. It is called "pride in your work," or "keeping your word" or "honesty." But you can also call it reliability, for that is the word your customer will have in mind when he thinks about you.

For Successful Selling—Understand Yourself

HOW TO DEVELOP RELIABILITY

Is reliability such a difficult character trait to develop?

Not at all. It does mean that if you make a statement, you must mean it. If you make a promise, you must keep it. It also means you will not make any promises if you have mental reservations. You will have the courage to say no to a customer's demand for a promise if you aren't sure you can keep the promise.

Your customers must learn that your interest extends beyond the sale, and that as far as you are concerned, the sale does not end when money and goods exchange hands.

HOW DO YOU KNOW IF YOU ARE RELIABLE?

Can you assume you are reliable? Can you disregard this important personality characteristic, take it for granted? Absolutely not! The proof is in the doing. You must prove your reliability not only to your customer but to yourself, and the way to do this is to be reliable. When you make a promise during a sale, keep it. Don't try to ease out of it by attributing a different or special meaning to what you said. You are a salesman, not a lawyer or a judge or an expert in semantics. Your interpretation of what you said isn't important, anyway. It's the interpretation of the customer that counts.

Reliability isn't a personality trait you can acquire overnight. It must mean something to you, and when it finally does, it will mean something to your customer. The ultimate proof will be customers who always come back, who always place repeat orders with you, or else who recommend you to other prospective customers. It means customers who ask for you by name in preference to other salesmen. Don't think the company

You Can Become A Super Salesman

employing you will be blind to this. They probably know the attributes of a good salesman better than you do. Reliability is one of the ways smart salesmen build up a loyal following, ensure customer satisfaction, and thereby guarantee their own selling success.

THE MOST WANTED PERSONALITY CHARACTERISTICS

Naturally, reliability is not the only important character trait. Although reliability is essential, there are other characteristics that also deserve attention. These include honesty, courage, sociability, enthusiasm, clarity of expression, sincerity, confidence, and ambition. Incidentally, none of these characteristics are sharp, distinct, or separated from each other. Consider how honesty ties in with reliability. If you make a promise to deliver on a certain date, and you do so, you could call it reliability, but it is also honesty.

These are characteristics we all have to a greater or lesser degree. The difference is that a successful salesman has consciously developed some or all of them to a considerable degree.

HONESTY

What does honesty mean?

Honesty can mean many things. It can mean not stealing or cheating. It can also mean being truthful and making out a report that is accurate down to the last penny. Our objective, however, is to make you into a salesman or saleswoman—not a saint. In the context of selling, honesty means the ability to make your sales pitch without making false claims.

This isn't as easy to do as it sounds.

For Successful Selling——Understand Yourself

Consider the list of desirable character traits for salesmen and you will see enthusiasm has been included. Now here is where some salesmen exhibit an unfortunate weakness, for they have an excess of enthusiasm and a shortage of honesty. You should be enthusiastic about the product you are selling or else you should look around for a different item. But if your product is good enough for you to be enthusiastic about, then there is no reason not to have an honest sales pitch!

Now everyone, at some time or another, tells a lie. But if you cannot describe your product in a straightforward and above-board manner, you will be wasting your time. The reason for this is that unless you are a superb actor your customer will sense the dishonesty. Even if he does not see through the deception the first time, he will certainly be alert the next. The old saying about honesty being the best policy may be worn out but that doesn't change the fact it is still true.

THE SUPER-HONEST SALESMAN

Honesty is an extremely difficult thing to define. It is possible to tell a lie without saying a word. A person can be dishonest by failing to do or say something as much as by doing or telling a lie. Lies range all the way from little white ones you may tell to spare someone's feelings to those that are out-and-out whoppers.

Being honest in salesmanship does *not* mean you are under any obligation to describe what you consider to be the weaknesses of your product. The old rule of "let the buyer beware" holds true. A salesman emphasizes his product's good qualities; he downplays his product's poor ones. If your customer asks if your product will last ten years, and it has an average life expectancy of one year, tell him so. But if your prospect assumes that what he is buying will last forever, there is no reason for you to tell him that it will not, if the subject does not arise during the sale.

THE SALES PITCH DISCOUNT

Many people are suspicious of salesmen and tend to discount some of what they say. Does this mean you should exaggerate in order to compensate for this credibility discount? No. You don't know whether the prospect believes 100 percent of what you say, or 80 percent or 50 percent so your safest course is to describe your product honestly. This means emphasizing all its good qualities, and calling them to the attention of the prospect. There is nothing dishonest in this. Keep in mind that many customers want to be sold, they want to be convinced, and many of them will meet you more than halfway. After a sale has been made and the product has been delivered to the customer, he may exaggerate or overstate the qualities of the product. That's his business, and if it does bring you additional sales, you have nothing to worry about. Your own honesty in selling is a big enough challenge without getting involved in some very deep soul searching.

COURAGE

Courage is included on the list of desirable characteristics for salesmen. What has courage to do with selling?

Courage is an absolutely necessary personality characteristic for salesmen. We are not speaking of courage in the usual sense, but rather the courage to go out and try to sell, day after day, with constant rebuffs. It takes guts to develop a successful selling technique. It is sometimes more politely known as determination. If you can face a day of trying to sell, when all your preceding days have been failures, you have courage.

ACQUIRING COURAGE

Because courage is such a tough characteristic it is much more difficult to acquire than some other personality characteristic, such as honesty. How do you acquire courage? Learn more about yourself. The toughest part of selling, incidentally, isn't facing the customer, but facing yourself. If you get downhearted, discouraged, worried, or fearful about your lack of sales, then you are at the point to prove whether you have courage or not. If you go out and still plug away at selling, you have courage. If you make all sorts of rationalizations and excuses, then you don't have it. You can have a hundred reasons for *not* going out to sell: it's raining; you don't feel too well; nobody will buy on Wednesday (or Thursday, or Friday); it's too far to travel; you don't have enough time, and so forth.

Does this mean a successful salesman never gets discouraged, never worries? Not a chance. But the salesman with courage takes all the poor selling days, the cranky customers, the unreasonable customers, the too demanding customers in his stride. He knows he must keep trying and he tries to learn from his failures. If he doesn't sell, he places the blame on himself not his customer. He challenges his sales pitch. He tries to analyze what went wrong and how to prevent it from happening again in the future.

He doesn't waste his time or energy in reproaching himself or in self-pity. Instead, he directs his thinking toward honest self-analysis.

Quite often, the difference between selling success and selling failure is very small. And a good salesman—the honest salesman—knows this. There will be days when not even the best salesman will be able to come home with sales. If this can happen to salesmen with years and years of experience, why should you be an exception?

THE MEANING OF COURAGE

While we use the word courage, perhaps we don't mean courage at all. Perhaps we mean being realistic and facing the world as it really is. You can take some comfort in the fact that there are tremendous numbers of mediocre, average salesmen. All it takes is just a little more effort on your part to be better than most, but this is something you must do for yourself!

SOCIABILITY

The next word on our list is sociability. Sociability means you must like people. No one is asking you to love all the people all the time. There will always be some people whom you dislike. On the average, however, you should like people enough to want to be with them, to enjoy talking to them, and to like mingling with them. A man can be either a hermit or a salesman; he can't be both!

Is it easy to like people? That depends. When we talk about people we talk about imperfect creatures. People lie, cheat, distort facts, fail to keep promises, are late for appointments, say one thing and mean another, and you could probably extend this list so it would fill several pages. But, if in spite of all their faults and disadvantages, you still like people and you are willing to accept them as they are, then you are sociable.

If you are critical, snobbish, stand-offish, highly selective, choosy, or are convinced you are superior to all other people in every respect, then

For Successful Selling—Understand Yourself

150

also consider you are missing one of the most important characteristics that lead to superior salesmanship—sociability.

WHAT SOCIABILITY IS NOT

For the salesman, sociability doesn't mean a poker game every Saturday night, or spending night after night in a bar. It doesn't mean being the life of the party. It doesn't mean being a soft touch for every hard luck story that comes along. You could do all these things and still not be sociable or have the kind of sociability that makes for good salesmanship. A salesman who enjoys talking to his customers, likes to meet them, gets satisfaction out of the "give and take" of a sale, regards selling as exciting because it gives him the opportunity to meet so many people is a sociable salesman. A good salesman can be sociable and yet never even consider fraternizing with his prospects. A sociable salesman doesn't yawn in his customer's face, not because it would be an impolite thing to do, but because he likes meeting new people to such an extent that it doesn't occur to him to be bored. And if he isn't bored, he won't act that way.

ENTHUSIASM

Enthusiasm isn't limited to a product. One reason so many salesmen like their work is the freedom and independence that go with it. In most jobs a worker is dependent on his boss, but in selling, the boss is dependent on the salesman. The more successful the salesman is, the more independent he can be. A good salesman doesn't worry about layoffs, or a business changing its location, or new management, or any other changes.

You Can Become A Super Salesman

A salesman's enthusiasm is in two parts. It exists for the product he is selling, and it exists for his job. Because he creates his own security, the salesman develops a sense of sureness. He is aware of his ability and knows that it is needed. He knows he can keep developing his sales ability to make himself and his work more and more wanted and valuable. He develops enormous self-confidence. Some people call this self-confidence by another name—enthusiasm.

A SALESMAN CAN BE AN INDEPENDENT BUSINESSMAN

In many cases a salesman works as an independent businessman. He sets his own hours, but this doesn't mean he starts at noon and finishes work in an hour or two. Most successful salesmen put in more than the usual salaried worker's 9 to 5 day. But the salesman doesn't complain because he likes his job, knows he is working for himself, and likes the feeling of independence. He also knows that he can determine his own earning power. Good salesmen are the key factor in most businesses and they are always in demand. A good salesman isn't concerned over the fact that he is approaching middle age or is getting past it; age is no barrier. Many businesses that set a hiring limit at 45 will hire salesmen of all ages. A good salesman can be between 16 and 65 years old. As long as a salesman produces sales, his age is his own business.

IT TAKES WORK TO BE A SUCCESSFUL SALESMAN

It may seem that we have painted a rosy picture about salesmanship, maybe so. But if salesmanship is so wonderful, if it can provide independence and rich rewards, why aren't people forming lines to become salesmen and saleswomen? Why are there so many help-wanted

For Successful Selling—Understand Yourself

ads for salesmen and saleswomen? Why are so many businesses concerned with selling willing to hire beginners, while most other businesses demand experience?

The answer is simple.

Selling is hard work. It is the only job in the world in which you can stand or fall, based only on your own efforts; it is the only job in the world in which you can blame failure only on yourself; and it is probably the only job in which you must use self-discipline. It is one of the few jobs you must take home with you so that you can perfect your selling techniques in the form of an improved sales pitch. It is one of the few jobs where you can work week after week and have little or no income to show for it. It is one of the few jobs where you must take an enormous amount of guff from complete strangers.

Selling is one of the few jobs where you must train yourself to get up early in the morning to do an honest day's work. It isn't easy to get out of bed when you know there is no one who cares whether you are early or late.

There is just one other fact. Make no mistake about it; salesmen do work and they work hard, and the best salesmen work harder than all the others.

But they know they are building something. Call it independence, a career, income, or whatever else you like.

SIMPLICITY

Simplicity is a word that just seems to demand an explanation. What is simplicity, and what has simplicity to do with selling?

Simplicity means being yourself.

But aren't you yourself? Not if you are acting a role. Not if you are putting on an act for your customers. Not if you hear the sound of your own voice. Not if you use words that really don't belong to you.

The opposite of simplicity means performing a part that is playacting and being someone else. Normally, in conversation we use simple words and simple sentences. People do this when they are more interested in communicating than in impressing others. If a person uses unusual or long words, or involved or flowery language, he isn't really being himself. He is evading simplicity. If a salesman is more interested in impressing the customer than in selling the product, he is avoiding simplicity. If the salesman tries to make the customer feel inferior, he is running away from simplicity.

There are two good reasons why simplicity is so important in selling. To sell you must communicate, and the most effective way of communicating is to use short, simple, direct language. The object of selling is to sell—not to impress the customer with how wonderful or superior you are, how well-educated, or what a wonderful command of the English language you have. The important factor in your conversation is the product you are selling—not you. You are talking to a customer, not to hear yourself talk, but to sell. This is a basic rule in selling, and right now is the best time for you to be aware of it.

IMPRESSING THE CUSTOMER

But isn't it your job to impress the customer?

No! It's your job to sell. If you try to demonstrate how wonderfully smart you can be, your customer will resent you and rightly so, for in effect you are calling him stupid. He really may be stupid, but he will still be smart enough not to buy from you.

The best thing to do is be yourself. Talk to your customer using the language that is normal and comfortable for you. Don't use technical words you may not understand or that may be beyond the understanding of your customer. Remember, also, that just because you know how your product works doesn't mean you are smarter—it just means you had a chance to learn about it before the customer. A good salesman likes to demonstrate a product, not because he wants to show how much he knows but because he is sincerely interested in getting this information across to his customer. A good salesman is more like a teacher than a preacher.

SINCERITY

We could possibly have omitted the word sincerity since it is included in the word honesty. A sincere salesman won't make a promise he knows he can't keep. Sincerity is made up of a lot of things. It means being on time for appointments, supplying samples when you say you will have them, and delivering merchandise on or before the day on which you have promised delivery. Sincerity means your sales pitch is made up of more than just words, that you know what you are saying, and that you don't plan to hide behind a dozen different excuses for failure to live up to your promises. When you make a sale, the entire burden of fulfillment is upon you. Your customer has no choice but to accept what you say in good faith.

Where does sincerity begin and honesty leave off?

You can't separate the two!

Is sincerity important? You had better believe it! Your beginning years in selling are your testing years. They are the years in which your customers evaluate you—size you up. They are the years in which your customers are going to decide whether you are sincere or not, whether they can rely on you, whether you make or break promises. They are the years in which your reputation will be growing or faltering.

Sincerity is a yardstick by which others measure you. You judge others by their sincerity, so it should come as no surprise that others judge you as well. And, of all people, a salesman is the one who is most open to this sort of evaluation.

It takes many years to build a reputation as a dependable salesman. When you do achieve that reputation, however, you will find many individuals and companies will prefer working with you, even though other product lines may tempt them. Very few buyers for companies like to take chances. That isn't the name of their game. You will be known for what you are and people will buy—or not buy—from you accordingly.

CONFIDENCE

What is confidence?

Confidence is the sureness a salesman has in his own ability. Confidence means a salesman has met all the challenges of salesmanship and has met them successfully. Confidence is the sureness a salesman has in his own ability. A good salesman knows he has chosen the right career, enjoys his career, and gets a sense of satisfaction from his work.

But none of us is born with confidence, and you can be sure that every star salesman started without it. You acquire confidence as you go along. Confidence is built on developing a sales pitch that's successful. Confidence means being able to sell more today than you did yesterday and being certain you will sell more tomorrow than you did today.

In a way, confidence is a reward you will get for doing your job right.

For Successful Selling—Understand Yourself

AMBITION

Anyone can be a salesman—of sorts. There are many salesmen and saleswomen who are satisfied to make a bare living; they aren't interested in getting ahead. To them selling is just another job, and, given the opportunity, they wouldn't mind at all doing something else. They are never ready for selling opportunities when they come along for the simple reason that they aren't prepared.

If this is your selling competition, and some of it is, then all you need do is to be just a little bit better. Right?

Wrong!

There are also salesmen and saleswomen who are ambitious, who do everything in their power to get ahead, who constantly try to improve their abilities, and who are always ready for opportunity when it comes along. This is your real competition. This represents the small but effective group who can take your sales away from you, who work as hard as you do, and who are determined to get as great a share of the selling market as possible.

What is ambition? There are many definitions, but one of the better ones defines it as a driving force. In effect, it means you are dissatisfied; you know you can make a better life for yourself, and you are determined to do so.

Ambition means doing everything you can possibly do to improve yourself in your selling profession. It means reading trade journals on selling, attending sales meetings, talking to other salesmen, and looking forward to your job.

At the start your competition will be the low-level salesman; but, as you improve, as you progress, as you develop your selling ability and begin to earn more and more, you will come into competition with those to whom selling is not only a career but a constant challenge.

You Can Become A Super Salesman

Ambition in selling is the force that makes you prepare a sales pitch. It is the force that makes you improve that sales pitch until it is as perfect as you can make it. It is the force that makes you change some of your personal characteristics and habits so they do not stand in the way of your selling success.

OTHER PERSONALITY CHARACTERISTICS

The topic of personality characteristics alone could occupy several chapters. For example, it is important for a salesman to be courteous; that is, treat the customer as though he were your personal guest. Don't say anything or do anything that will embarrass him. Don't call attention to any of his physical shortcomings. People are very sensitive about their weight, height, shape, lack of hair, and so forth.

Courtesy is also a matter of common sense. Don't smoke when you are making a sales pitch. Even if your customer smokes, you should not. Even a chain smoker doesn't enjoy having someone else's smoke blown into his face. Don't chew gum when you are selling. If you have a nervous habit, such as pulling your hair, picking at your face or teeth, do it in the privacy of your own home, but not when you face a customer. Courtesy includes politeness and consideration. The fact that a customer is impolite to you, chews gum or smokes, or has an annoying nervous habit does not mean you have the same privileges.

WHAT'S NEXT

In this chapter you have been given some suggestions about several of the most important personality characteristics of a good salesman.

For Successful Selling—Understand Yourself

Learning more about yourself and understanding more about yourself is essential. Quite often a salesman will find his sales blocked, not by the customer's refusal to buy, not because of an unsatisfactory product, but simply because the salesman has blocked it.

With the world so full of people who are ready to be antagonistic, why be your own worst enemy?

You must not only understand yourself, but you must also do whatever you possibly can to understand your customers. This may not be so easy, since your contact with the customer will generally be short and, unless the customer is a repeat type, your opportunity for analyzing, understanding, and appreciating the kind of personality your customer has will be extremely limited. And yet, as you will see, it is possible to set up some sort of classification for people and to put them into groups. An experienced salesman becomes a good judge of human nature.

FOR SUCCESSFUL SELLING—
UNDERSTAND YOUR CUSTOMERS

What is a sale?

A sale means many things, and many definitions have been given to it. Consider a sale as a human challenge, a challenge to you. In effect, a sale is one person communicating with another. Consequently, success in selling will be closely related to the way you understand people, your interest in them, and your curiosity in learning how they think and why they act the way they do.

No two people are alike. This means that as a salesman it would be useless to use the same approach when trying to sell to a housewife or a businessman. With a businessman you might talk about the economic value of the product. You realize he knows how to handle and deal with salesmen, that he can analyze a business proposal, and that his main interest is the profit opportunity your product offers him. You also review the secondary benefits of the product you are selling, such as personal satisfaction and prestige in a way which would clearly indicate their business value. With the businessman your approach will be direct and to the point for you know his time is worth money. If you waste his time, your chances of making a sale are slim and the opportunity for coming back again for a repeat sale will be very small. The sales appeal you will make to the businessman should be factual: Your product will create a profit for him; it will sell well; it is backed by the reputation and integrity of your company; the product is advertised and promoted. The businessman does not see himself as personally involved in the product. He has no emotional relationship to it.

Now consider sales to an entirely different type of customer—a housewife. Although she may appreciate the economic considerations involved, she will place greater emphasis on the comfort, satisfaction, or the time-saving benefits the product can offer her. Also, she will not overlook the added prestige gained by owning your product. The housewife will become involved with the product and will make a purchase only if she can relate to it on a personal level. Her viewpoint is less detached than that of the businessman, and she is susceptible to an emotional approach.

These two examples demonstrate that in dealing with the general public, you must place yourself in the position of an observer, try to classify people according to types, and then study the most efficient ways to sell each type. Your selling efforts and selling success will depend on

You Can Become A Super Salesman

how well you understand each of the types that make up the general public. While both selling approaches are successful (the one to the businessman and the one to the housewife), they are not interchangeable. A businessman might be repelled by an emotional approach; the housewife would regard the sales pitch you used for the businessman with distaste.

Although here we have presented two distinctly different types, the problem is that you cannot always sell to such completely clear-cut groups. While a particular social group may have typical traits or characteristics, the individuals who compose that same group probably hold a wide variety of viewpoints. Indiscriminate generalizations of people may lead you to mistakes much larger than failing to understand a general type.

ADDRESSING THE CUSTOMER

Your first step in making a sale is to look at your customer. But don't you need to do this anyway? How can you make a sale, other than a mail order sale, if you don't look at the prospect? Strangely enough it is entirely possible to look at a person and not see him.

The trouble lies in the word "look." Perhaps a better word would be "evaluate." When you are about to make a sale, you must make yourself fully conscious of the individual to whom you address your sales pitch. This will tell you, or it should, whether or not your sales effort is effective. By visually evaluating your prospect, you accomplish several things. First, you will be able to determine what type of person you are addressing. The sales pitch for a businessman is different from the one used for a housewife. The sales approach for a man is different from the

For Successful Selling—Understand Your Customers

one used for a woman. Your sales pitch should also be influenced by the way in which the prospect is dressed, his age, what he says and how he says it, and his facial expressions.

But why bother evaluating your prospect? Why not move right ahead with your sales pitch and let your potential customer decide whether or not he wants to buy? The answer is simple. Your time is worth money, and if you are working on a commission basis, you will want to make the most sales over a given period of time. "Sizing up" your customers will help you do this.

There is still another reason why you must evaluate your customers, that is, recognize his type immediately. Some people are time wasters. They may have nothing to do, may be trying to kill time, and may regard your selling efforts as a form of entertainment—entertainment for which you pay and is free to them. Some people are also habitual shoppers. They know what they want to buy, they know just what they want to spend, probably right down to the last penny, and so they really aren't prospects. The successful salesman is one who knows two things: how not to waste his time, and how not to let anyone else waste his time. Both points are equally important.

CLASSIFICATION ACCORDING TO NEED

Why is it important to "know your customer" (a professional way of saying identify each customer according to type, such as businessman, housewife, doctor, clerk, engineer, lawyer, or actor)? The two most important reasons are that you must speak in terms of the prospect's interest and appeal to your prospect in terms of his needs.

You Can Become A Super Salesman

THE PROSPECT'S INTERESTS

We have given you two examples of speaking in terms of your prospect's interest: the businessman and the housewife. Now imagine you are going to sell a set of books to a doctor. How would you speak to him in terms of his own interest? Perhaps you would mention that the books would help him relax. They may lend a distinguished air to his waiting room. He may want to use the books for reference.

If you are selling the same set of books to a housewife, however, you might point out that one or two of these books on the coffee table in her living room would add to the appearance of the room, or, if placed in a bookcase, they would make the room look more distinguished. You might discuss the richness of the bindings, the attractive colors of the covers, topics, by the way, that might not be of great interest to the doctor.

Note that you are selling the same product, but to two different types of customers, and therefore you use different selling approaches.

CREATIVE SELLING

On the other hand, if your prospect has no need for what you offer, you must learn how to create that need. You can do this by demonstrating a product's benefits and its application in solving some of the customer's problems. Take as an example the salesman who sold a number of heating units in Brazil to be used in coffee dryers, which had previously used log fires and exposure to the sun. He concluded an almost impossible sale and at the same time offered the customer substantial cost savings. That's creative selling.

Creative selling is contained in your sales pitch, or it should be.

For Successful Selling—Understand Your Customers

Electric refrigerators replaced the old wooden icebox because a need for them was created. In terms of the product you are selling, you must take some time to think of how to create a desire for it. If you are selling a vacuum cleaner, for example:

1. It cleans the house faster.
2. It makes the house really clean because it gets all the dirt other cleaners leave behind.
3. It cuts down on the amount of work the housewife must do.
4. It is much less tiring because the cleaner is light and can be easily carried from room to room.
5. A housewife will not get her hands or clothes dirty when she empties the cleaner.
6. With this cleaner the housewife never needs to bend or stoop.
7. The long handle that comes with the cleaner is covered with a soft material and the housewife's hands will never become rough even though the cleaner is used often.

These suggestions may only be suitable for a vacuum cleaner, but the product you are selling may have any number of advantages. The only requirement for making such a list is to think about and get to know your product. Remember, this list of advantages accomplishes one very important objective: it arouses a feeling of need for the product in the mind of the prospective customer.

THERE MUST BE A NEED

There are people who will say about a product, "Who wants it? Who needs it?" These statements exist because no salesman has answered the objections. A creative salesman, however, can create a need. No creative salesman is ever stumped by the question, "What do I need it for?" He will have half a dozen answers ready, not when he is trying to make the sale, but long before it. He will consider this objection when he is preparing his sales pitch. An important part of your previously prepared sales pitch, then, consists of all the possible reasons why a customer should buy your product. The customer will need your product because: it will save him money; it will be more convenient to use; it will outperform the product he is using now; and it will cut down on his work. These are just a few of the general ideas you can use to create a need in the mind of the customer.

Most of us want things, but we are not born wanting them. The desire to have material benefits is stimulated by the society in which we live. Every advertisement you read is an attempt to create a "want" on your part. Every ad you hear on radio or that you see on television contains reminders about something you need. The magazine, radio, and television ads never assume that the reader or listener has a need. They try to create the need. Read, listen, and look more carefully the next time you come in contact with ads. Note that the ad usually states that the product:

1. Offers great savings. (This reminds the prospect of the need to save.)
2. Cuts down on work time. (We can all use work time for some other purposes.)
3. Is convenient. (We need items that are more convenient than the product we are now using.)
4. Is popular with many people. (Our neighbors probably have one therefore we need to have the same product.)

A salesman is somewhat like an advertisement. An advertisement creates a need in order to sell a product. The salesman, though, has the unique advantage over the advertisement of being able to talk directly to the prospect. He can create the need while the prospect waits. Selling,

For Successful Selling—Understand Your Customers

then, has two basic parts: creating a need and convincing a customer that your product will fill that need.

HOW TO DISCOVER INTERESTS AND NEEDS

Suppose you meet a prospect "cold." How would you discover his interests and needs?

Think about it.

The answer is: you must engage him in conversation. Consider just how you can talk to a customer with the intention of discovering his interests and, at the same time, letting him know about your product.

The prospect is talking to you because he wishes to:

1. Feel important
2. Impress others with his importance
3. Be praised
4. Express his opinion
5. Be with others who know something about him
6. Gain goodwill
7. Be appreciated
8. Talk about his hobby, his work, his interests
9. Have his thoughts appreciated
10. Feel comfortable and at ease

Note that we have not said anything as yet about the product you are selling or about the needs of the prospect. Most initial contacts between a salesman and a customer do not permit the salesman to launch immediately into his sales pitch. But while the salesman should not begin the conversation with the product, the customer might start off with, "I'm interested in getting. . . ,'' Or I would like to buy. . . ,'' or ''I'm shopping around for a. . .'' During the time the customer is making this opening statement, you should look at the customer and note if the customer is:

1. Old
2. Young
3. More important in rank or authority than you
4. Less important in rank or authority than you
5. Person of another sex
6. Well-dressed or poorly dressed
7. Well-groomed or poorly groomed

Conversations with each type of these speakers take different approaches.

OLDER PEOPLE

You must realize that old people are probably more experienced than you, so don't try to impress them with your experience. Keep in mind that no one enjoys being considered old. Remember also that the older person enjoys being consulted about his ideas, experiences, and opinions. Elderly persons enjoy talking and like to take complete control of a conversation. Let them do so. Gradually move the conversation around to your product.

Elderly people are often retired and find time moving slowly, so be careful. You have a sale in mind; they want conversation. They have a tendency to wander away from the subject, so it will be up to you not to let yourself be drawn away.

For Successful Selling—Understand Your Customers

YOUNGER PEOPLE

Keep your guard up at all times, young people can be aggressive. With young people who want to act older, do not argue or insist on your rights; however, be firm. Show interest in what appears to interest your prospect. With young people the sale can move along more rapidly than the slower pace you must use with an older person. Don't emphasize how long your product will last, for this topic isn't generally of interest to them. They will relate very strongly and be interested in your product if they can relate to it.

MORE IMPORTANT IN RANK OR AUTHORITY

This is one of the most difficult types for a salesman to handle. You should maintain your own independence of thought, but do not be belligerent. You should be both respectful and firm. You should allow the customer to lead the conversation. You should listen more and speak less. Explain your product and talk about its advantages, but do not argue. Be quick, open, and sincere with your answers. Act naturally. People of this type are accustomed to giving orders and expect their orders to be followed. If, for example, your product comes in different colors, they will order the color they want without first asking if other colors are available. They will not ask for a delivery date, but will specify it, assuming that delivery will be made at their convenience. The price of the product you are selling will be of interest to them, but they will not argue about it. They generally know what they want and have made up their mind well in advance. If they do have any doubts, it will be to decide which of two different items to buy, not whether they should buy or not.

You Can Become A Super Salesman

LESS IMPORTANT IN RANK OR AUTHORITY

Customers of this type look up to the salesman as a figure of authority. They are often shy and hesitate to approach a salesman. They are frequently fearful of making a purchase. They worry about price, and it is a subject they will bring up early in the conversation. They are not accustomed to having their wishes respected. It is easy to create a need for your product with this type of customer. They generally do not make unreasonable demands. It is essential to make them feel comfortable and calm. Show interest in what they say and encourage them to speak. Be dignified, but courteous and kind, and be careful not to say anything that might possibly be interpreted as being offensive.

SELLING TO A PERSON OF A DIFFERENT SEX

Women tend to shift from one topic to another very rapidly. Be prepared for this, and don't try to stop it. Women often talk more than men. Remember the purpose of the opening conversation; it is to find out the interests and needs of your prospect. To do this, you must avoid a long or rambling conversation, therefore direct the conversation through the use of questions and answers.

For the most part, women relate very strongly to the products they buy. They do not see themselves as separate from the product, but directly connected or a part of it. They are color conscious, style conscious, and fashion conscious. They are as concerned about the beauty of a product as they are about its usefulness. They are seldom technically oriented. If you are selling vacuum cleaners, for example, a description of the motor's horsepower will not mean much; they will, however, be interested in its superior cleaning ability. Women are

For Successful Selling—Understand Your Customers

generally not as physically strong as men and so the weight of a product or its ease in handling is important to them. They are also impressed with products that seldom need repair or that can be easily serviced. Women enjoy shopping and have a tendency to spend more time doing so. They may be accompanied by other women whom they will consult with about the merits of your product.

If you are selling to a man you will find he is more oriented toward technical terms. The horsepower rating of a motor means more to him than a statement about better cleaning ability. Men seldom have as much shopping patience as women, they like to make decisions more quickly, they do not often call on others for advice, and they frequently shop alone. Unlike women, they are more utility and less style conscious. They tend to take a greater part in the conversation. They do not hesitate to express opinions, sometimes strongly. They are often interested in the strength or durability of items, rather than in outward appearance.

WELL-DRESSED OR POORLY DRESSED

The way in which a customer is dressed will give you a clue to your correct sales approach. If customers are well-dressed, you may be in a position to sell the higher priced articles in your product line. They are interested in saving money, but will pay a higher price if they feel they are getting value for their money. They tend to be more authoritative and are more accustomed to ordering rather than requesting. They often know what they want. While they may seem rather determined, they are polite and well-mannered. They often speak well and are sometimes surprisingly knowledgeable about the products you are selling. They tend to be motivated by newspaper and magazine advertising.

Poorly dressed customers are quite the opposite. They often do not know what they want, or aren't sure. One of the earliest questions they ask is the price. They tend to move toward the lower cost line of products and are frequently concerned with the possible life of the product and the cost of repairs. They are not as insistent on color or style and prefer utility to fashion. They tend to look up to salesmen if they are women; they may be slightly hostile if they are men.

WELL-GROOMED OR POORLY GROOMED

This category is similar to the well-dressed or poorly dressed group. The well-dressed are well-groomed, while the poorly dressed are often, but not always, poorly groomed. The well-groomed are sure of themselves, know what they want, will ask about price but often do not argue about it. They may speak well and make their wants known clearly. They are interested in obtaining value. Those who are poorly groomed often may not always know what they want. They are more interested in utility rather than in style or fashion.

GENERALIZATIONS

The statements we have made about the various types of customers are subject to all sorts of exceptions; they are only generalizations. An elderly person, for example, may make a purchase in a manner characteristic of a much younger one, or a well-dressed woman may seem indifferent to style or fashion. In time, however, you will be able to evaluate people rapidly. The important thing is not to prejudge someone on the basis of appearance alone. People often do not talk or think in a way that corresponds to their dress.

For Successful Selling—Understand Your Customers

QUESTIONS

Questions represent one of the salesman's greatest advantages, and by this we mean questions asked by both the customer and you. A customer's questions will give you a clear indication as to what the customer has in mind, that is, whether he has a particular need, and will also let you know how far along the customer may be in making a purchase before hearing what you have to say.

Not all customers ask questions. Some of them just let you handle the entire sale and ask few, if any, questions. In this case you can learn what you want to know by taking the initiative and asking them the questions.

Questions also allow you to determine whether or not a person has understood what you have said, and whether you have expressed yourself clearly. Be careful, however, some questions can be offensive, or may be considered as such. The purpose of a question is to help a sale along to its conclusion, and should not, innocently or otherwise, antagonize the prospect. Never ask a question such as, "Am I making myself perfectly clear?" If you are, the question is unnecessary. If you are not the customer may not admit it. You should be able to determine whether or not the customer understands you from the expression on his face or by what he says.

Don't fire a whole series of questions at the customer. He isn't in court and you aren't a cross-examining attorney. Space out your questions and do not ask one directly after another. Try to make the questions appear as though they would occur naturally in conversation. And, to avoid asking useless questions, make sure the questions relate directly to the product or to the sale. Don't ask questions that will annoy, embarrass, or irritate the customer. Don't ask questions of personal nature, unless such questions must be answered in connection with the product you are selling. Don't ask any questions that will force the customer to have a lower opinion of himself.

These restrictions on questions apply to you, not to the customer. He can ask any questions he likes, in any order he likes, and he can ask one after the other. These is no reason for a salesman ever to feel resentful about this. On the contrary, questions on the part of the customer are so valuable and helpful that most salesmen wish their customers would ask more, not fewer, of them.

ANSWERS

For every question, whether asked by you or by your customer, there should be an answer. An evasion of a question, or replying to a question in such a way that the customer does not get the information he wants can hurt the sale. The prospect's answers to your questions, plus the general conversation, will enable you to discover exactly what his needs are and where his interests lie. When asking questions, put the listener to the test. His answers disclose his inner self and his unfilled needs. In many sales procedures, the opening portion of the sale consists of questions and answers, with each side probing for information. After the questions have been satisfied by appropriate answers, the salesman can use the previously asked questions as a springboard from which to launch into a description of the product. This description is neither a monologue nor a speech. It should not be continuous. Give the customer a chance to talk, and even more important, to ask questions. Then use these questions to continue your sales pitch. In other words, make your prospect a part of the selling procedure. Don't exclude him from it lest he exclude you from the sale.

STARTING THE SALES PITCH

After the question and answer period you will have a much better knowledge of just what are your customer's needs. Start your sales pitch, but at this time modify it in terms of your particular customer. After all, the whole purpose of the previous question and answer period is that you do not waste your time, or your customer's time.

If you are first starting in sales, and are preparing your first sales pitch, you may need to use your imagination or else have a friend help you. Take an imaginary selling situation as the base on which to prepare your sales pitch. Then:

1. Select the best possible approach to follow, taking advantage of all the selling statements you can use most favorably.
2. Think of all the possible objections the customer might make.
3. Think of all the answers you can make to those objections.
4. Make your sales pitch in a reasonable amount of time.
5. Be sure to talk about essentials. Pay less attention to details. Details become important when the customer has expressed his willingness to buy. They indicate he has changed from a prospect to a buyer.
6. Don't talk aimlessly—get to the point.
7. If possible, make a demonstration.
8. Be sure to allow enough time for changes or corrections in your pitch, should this be necessary.
9. Use simple, clear, and precise language. Your customer may know more about the English language than you do.

You Can Become A Super Salesman

THE CUSTOMER'S REACTION

Assume you have passed a small question and answer period with the customer, and that you have made your sales pitch. Now the question is how will the customer react? What will he say or do? There are three possibilities:

First, the customer's reaction will be negative. He will indicate in some way that he isn't interested, that he doesn't need the product, that it isn't what he has in mind. He may say so or he may say nothing. He may simply show it in a disinterested attitude.

Second, the customer's reaction will be positive. He may not say so but will show it by his expression, or, quite often, by asking more specific questions about the product. These questions, unlike the earlier ones, will be more detailed. A question on delivery date, style, or operating instructions shows the customer has a definite interest and that his reaction is positive.

Third, the customer's reaction is neutral. He may or may not be interested in the product. Nothing you have said so far has aroused a feeling of need, and yet at the same time the customer may think the product could be of use to him. He just isn't sure.

During a sale, a customer will, even without wanting to, reveal his hidden thoughts about the article being offered. Human nature shows itself through movements of the body. Some customers are spontaneous in their actions and will show exactly what they think or feel. Their words will simply confirm the motions of their face or body. Other customers are cautious and jealously guard their thoughts. A customer of this type may deliberately be careful since he believes that lack of interest may help him get a better price. People who are cautious in their speech or body movements may not show interest deliberately to help their bargaining position. A good salesman must understand something of human nature and human behavior.

For Successful Selling—Understand Your Customers

There are clear indications when the customer is interested in your product. These are:
1. Certain words
2. Certain actions
3. Certain expressions

THE CUSTOMER'S WORDS

Customers will usually speak certain words or phrases that will reveal their interest or desire to buy the product you are selling. These are: Repeated or persistent questions on one or various points. The same questions may be asked in several different ways. If the question concerns delivery of the product you may hear:
1. When can you make delivery?
2. Are you sure delivery will be made on time?
3. What is the name of the shipping company?
4. Around what time of day will delivery be made?
5. Is the cost of delivery included in the purchase price?
6. Is the delivery covered by insurance?
7. Will the product be damaged during delivery?
8. Will shipment be made through a responsible carrier?
9. How will delivery be made? By truck? By train?

All of these questions are on the same theme. Naturally, you can't expect the customer to ask so many questions, but even just two or three along similar lines will indicate the customer is seriously considering a purchase.

Sometimes the customer will use words or phrases that express a direct and clear acceptance of the offer. "Yes," "True," "I am of the same opinion," "That's right," "I know that," "I'm aware of that,"

"It's quite clear," "Naturally," "You are right," "I agree." The customer will use just one of these phrases, and he may accompany it with some body movement to indicate acceptance, such as moving his head up and down to show a yes intention.

Another favorable indication consists of questions concerning guarantee or warranty. For example, "How long is the warranty period?" "Do you provide spares?" "Where can I have it repaired?" "Is the warranty for labor, for parts, or for both?" "When do I receive the warranty?" All of these questions indicate the customer has made up his mind to buy, but simply wants additional information.

Certain typical qualifications that are common should be considered favorable indications. As customers try to hide their enthusiasm for a product, they often make reservations or objections that, nevertheless, disclose their buying intentions. As an example, "Yes, but it doesn't have all the features I'm looking for." "There are quite a few of this type of product available." "It's not a bad product." "I've seen the same item sold elsewhere but at a lower price (or at a better discount, or in more attractive colors, or with different features, or with better features)."

CUSTOMER'S ACTIONS

There are certain actions on the part of the customer that are usually made when the customer has a real interest. When a salesman detects them he can be certain the customer is attracted to the product. These actions are: Careful inspection of the article. He takes it in his hands, looks at it carefully, tests the mechanism, operates it, tries it on, looks at himself in the mirror, inspects the packaging. Naturally, the customer doesn't do all these things. It all depends on the product you are selling.

For Successful Selling—Understand Your Customers

However, some or all of these actions are a form of persistent testing. They represent various experiments performed by the customer to assure himself of the quality of the product you are selling.

CUSTOMER'S EXPRESSIONS

The face is one of the most difficult parts of the human body to control. An experienced salesman knows he should watch his customer's face to find out if the product pleases him and just what his buying intentions are. As with everything else, you should learn how to interpret these indications because the customer is often aware that his face may easily give him away. Consequently, this is the part he tries to control. These expressions usually are: a bright face, knitted eyebrows (as though expressing deep concentration), a grin, tilting of the head, squinting, and slight upward curling of the lips.

Sales specialists maintain that a salesman should stop selling and start to close the sale the moment he detects one of these signs. This is similar to what a driver would do when facing a green light: he pays attention, gets ready, and starts to move. For the salesman, this is the time to hold back on words or actions that might delay the sale, or arguments and demonstrations that could lengthen it. He should only be concerned with closing the sale using a traditionally accepted technique, because the psychological or timely moment is at hand.

Questions on the part of the customer at this point could also show the customer's readiness to buy. But what if the customer does not ask questions at this time? Here you will have to rely on the customer's face to supply you with the answer. A smile on the customer's face, however small, would be one of the clues that the customer is ready to buy.

You Can Become A Super Salesman

THE SALESMAN'S REACTION

The salesman should also react to these various buying indications with words that will answer only what was asked by the customer. If the prospect has asked a typical warranty question, the salesman should answer this question specifically. Do not bring up any new selling ideas at this time. Say nothing that will cause the customer to start asking some new questions. If the customer is "sold," all you can do at this point by making additional selling efforts is to send the customer along on a detour away from the sale.

In short, then, the salesman must be alert to the prospect's reaction to his sales pitch. But suppose there's little or no reaction? Then there are ways in which you can stimulate it.

WAYS OF STIMULATING BUYING INDICATIONS

A salesman will often run through his presentation in a proper professional fashion without stimulating a single buying indication from the customer. There are some customers who either have no interest in what you are selling or who have tremendous self-control. Under the circumstances, you must learn what the customer is thinking to know if you should expand your conversation, ask more questions, continue a demonstration, or do something that will help your customer make up his mind.

Here the salesman has a great resource in the use of questions. What sometimes happens during a sale is that the customer becomes withdrawn. Instead of the give and take relationship that should exist between a salesman and the customer, the customer has cut the relationship during the time the salesman is making his sales pitch.

For Successful Selling—Understand Your Customers

There may be a number of reasons for this behavior. The customer may be afraid or unsure of the product or the salesman. The customer may be the type who is unable to pay attention more than a limited amount of time. Something about the salesman has affronted the customer. Something may have been said by the salesman during his sales pitch that triggered a negative reaction on the part of the customer. The true reason may have nothing to do with the salesman or the product, but may be some hidden psychological characteristic of the customer. Whatever the cause or reason, the salesman at this time can use questions to force the customer to take a more positive attitude. Typical questions that will compel the customer to a decision are:

> Which do you prefer, this or that?
> Shall we ship it to you or would you prefer to take it with you?
> Do you like this color or would you want a different one?
> Would you prefer the budget model or the deluxe unit?
> Will you take it as it is or would you wish to have it gift wrapped?
> Will this be cash or do you want to charge it?

Note one thing in common with all these questions. Not one of them gives the customer a chance to say no. Each of these questions assumes the customer has made a decision and that it is the customer's decision to buy. Every one of these questions is calculated to compel the customer to answer. Furthermore, he cannot answer with a single word, As we said earlier, he is not in a position to say no, but he cannot give a simple yes answer either. In replying to the question, then, the customer must disclose his way of thinking and in this way will reveal his true intentions. The salesman will then have available the information he needs to know just where he stands in relation to the sale. This questioning approach is often desirable, particularly with customers who are very much reserved.

STAGE SETTING THE DEMONSTRATION

Many demonstrations fail because the salesman is a good salesman. This may sound odd, but sometimes a salesman will have such faith and belief in his product that he will come to the conclusion that the product should sell itself. What has happened here is that the salesman is so good that he has sold himself.

Experienced salesmen know that while a quality product is essential, the use of a salesman is still needed. Furthermore, they know enough to show their products in the best possible light. Thus, a jewelry salesman will often show his products against a dark velvet background. A vacuum cleaner salesman found his sales increasing when the rug he was using for demonstration purposes was changed from drab to bright colors, and when he used colored paper scraps to pick up instead of bits of newspaper. A manufacturer of unpainted furniture found his sales increasing when he covered his samples with a clear plastic paint. This did not hide the wood grain, but made it shiny. Department stores often exhibit furniture in sample rooms designed by interior decorators. Manufacturers of liquor use elaborately designed packaging for extra sales during holidays. One salesman of fabrics deliberately shows fabrics of strongly contrasting colors at the same time to supply a dramatic emphasis for his demonstration. A refrigerator salesman is experimenting with panels of different colors as backdrops for his product to find out which color produces the most sales. One manufacturer's product is packaged so well that one salesman insists on opening the carton right in front of the customer. He tells his customers that a manufacturer who takes such care in packaging must be exceptionally proud of his product. Color, design, arrangement, style, new ideas—all of these can be used by the alert salesman in an effort to put his product (or products) forth in the most presentable way.

For Successful Selling—Understand Your Customers

THE IN-STORE SALESMAN

Some salesmen work in stores under an arrangement with the store owner or manager. The store does not pay the salesman's salary. Instead the store receives payment from the salesman for his use of a small section of the store area for exhibiting and selling the product. The salesman is now a businessman even though he is working on someone else's premises. To create sales, such a salesman must:

1. Attract the attention of buyers. Since buyers will be visiting all sections of the store and since many of them will have come into the store with the idea of buying a specific product, the salesman must do something to get their attention. He can do this by means of illuminated signs, active signs (signs that have moving parts), an attractive model, or by having a demonstration in progress. There will always be a few prospects who will have enough curiosity to stop and to listen.

2. Once the prospective buyer's attention has been caught, the salesman must next do whatever he can to stimulate the prospect's interest in his product. One salesman offers free samples, but never gets around to giving them away until he fully completes his sales pitch. Another salesman offers a well-known product at an extremely low price, but does not sell until he completes his pitch on the product he does want to sell.

3. During his sales presentation, the salesman does his best to arouse a desire or need on the part of the prospect.

4. During the sales presentation the salesman keeps his eyes on his prospects to determine the best moment at which to stop talking and to begin closing.

5. The final step is the sale itself.

Note how similar these steps are to those described earlier. In other

You Can Become A Super Salesman

words, although the product may be different, and although the circumstances under which the salesman does his job are different, the steps taken toward making a sale are the same as for other types of salesmen.

DIRECT SELLING

There are some businesses that seem to try to eliminate salesmen, but selling must still be done. This kind of selling is known as direct selling because the supplier or manufacturer makes direct contact with the consumer or his market.

Consider the case of a farmer. He can sell his products to a consumer cooperative or to some organization that will buy his entire output and then distribute it to markets, restaurants, and so forth. Sometimes the farmer will set up his own open-air road stand and sell his produce directly to transient travelers. The farmer does not become a salesman but rather is an order taker. He makes no effort to make sales for he does not know how to increase his sales. He is a farmer, not a salesman. He lets his customers pick and choose.

Another type of direct sales consists of selling directly to the consumer by mail. In this case a salesman is employed by the manufacturer, except he isn't known as such. He is an individual who is an expert in mail selling. This direct mail selling expert is actually a salesman who has specialized. He uses all the techniques of other salesmen. He attracts attention to his products; he arouses interest in them; he develops a need for his products; and he closes by selling. The only difference is that he does not see the customer and so relies on the power of the printed word. His disadvantage is that he does not see the customer and he does not know what the customer is thinking. Such salesmen keep very careful records of who buys their products, and they learn as much about their customers as they can. They sometimes ask their customers to fill out questionnaires that will supply them with useful information. The salesman does this to overcome the disadvantage of not being able to see the customer.

WHAT'S NEXT?

There is still one more point that must be described and it is probably the most important point of all—the close. The close means exactly what it says. It is the point at which the salesman knows his customer is ready to purchase.

This is a delicate moment in the sale. Many salesmen dread this part of selling more than any other because they know that a wrong word or a wrong question can undo all their selling efforts. Many salesmen are afraid of closing because they simply do not know how. The next chapter discusses closing techniques in detail.

THE FINAL STEP—
CLOSING THE SALE

Just how important is closing the sale in the selling process? To answer this question, consider what you are trying to do. You are trying to make a sale. You have previously prepared your sales pitch. You have become thoroughly acquainted with your product. You have learned as much as you can about competing products. You are prepared to "size up" your customer so you know as much as possible about him. You are ready to answer all questions. You know the value of the customer's questions, and you have a few previously prepared questions of your own. You have practiced demonstrating the product until you can do it blindfolded.

Then what is left?

Just one final step—the close. The termination of the sale. The action in which the customer pays, or agrees to buy, and you complete a sales slip or order form for the customer's signature. In short, then, the close is precisely that. The finish of the sale, but on a successful basis. You have now earned your salary, or your commission, or a combination of both. You have not only acquired some earnings, but something money cannot buy—a small amount of self-confidence, the reward of adequate preparation.

All of the steps mentioned above—the preparation, the questions, the product examination—all of these steps do not have meaning unless you know how to close the sale. If you do not or if you cannot perform this final selling action, then all of the preceding steps are meaningless.

WHEN TO CLOSE

There are two steps in closing any sale: knowing when to close and using the correct procedure in closing. But what about guiding the sale toward the close? Actually, that is what you have been doing from the moment the sale started; from the beginning of the dialogue you have been having with your sales prospect. The whole purpose of selling is that of guiding the prospect toward the close.

There are many salesmen who are really not very good salesmen for a simple reason, they never learned how to close. They may follow every one of the other steps in selling and follow them through aggressively. They may be diligent in locating prospects; they may have spent considerable time in developing a good sales pitch; and they may present that sales pitch with enthusiasm. But if they have no understanding of how to close a sale, then all of their efforts are wasted. It is sad to consider such useless effort, but that's why we are emphasizing it now.

You Can Become A Super Salesman

A salesman cannot omit any of the important steps in making a sale, and he cannot afford to omit the final and most essential of all the steps—closing.

CLOSING FACTORS

Unfortunately, closing a sale isn't all that simple. If you try to close too early, the prospect may pull away from you and in so doing develop considerable sales resistance. He may get a temporary mental block against buying that will be difficult, if not impossible, to overcome. The prospect must be "purchase ready," that is, he must be at the psychologically correct point before he will buy.

On the other hand, if you delay the close too long, if you go beyond the "purchase ready" point, the prospect may get some second thoughts about buying. Your sales arguments will have lost some of their effectiveness. The prospect may become bored or tired and may begin to wonder whether he should buy or not. Some of his buying enthusiasm will have disappeared. Some salesmen are often baffled at this point because a prospect, seemingly ready to buy, has terminated the selling discussion with a "Well, I'll think about it and let you know." What this really means is, "I've thought about it and the answer is no."

When to close depends on two people.

You are one of them and the prospective buyer is the other. If your attitude is that closing depends entirely on the prospect, then you will either not close any sales or not close as many as you should. To say that closing depends only on the prospect is just a way of shirking or avoiding a selling responsibility. It is an excuse used by salesmen who, for one reason or another, do not know how or are unwilling to close.

The Final Step—Closing the Sale

Of course, it is important and essential for your prospect to say yes. But he will not say yes unless you act accordingly, that is, unless you lead him to the point where he wants to buy what you are selling and indicates his readiness to give you an order. And so, what is important in the act of selling is not exactly the prospect, or the commercial conditions, but you—the salesman—the man who goes after a sale and closes it successfully.

TIMING THE CLOSE

No two salesmen really agree on when to close. Some salesmen believe it should follow logically after making the demonstration, after making the sales pitch, and after answering all questions about the product. In other words, they look on it as a logical ending.

However, there are some salesmen who begin their close almost at once. Within minutes after starting a discussion with a prospect, they assume the sale has been completed, even though they may still be engaged in a question and answer period and even before they have made a demonstration. One successful salesman who uses this method takes out his order book and after some preliminary but short discussion keeps the order book out in the open where the prospect can see it. At an appropriate moment near the beginning of the sale the salesman asks for the prospect's name, address, phone number, and some other data and stops the entire sale while writing slowly and carefully in the order book. This gesture isn't lost on the prospect. He believes that somewhere along the line he indicated that he would make the purchase. Other salesmen feel this procedure is too strong. Instead, they take out their order book and keep it where the prospect can see it. After the sales pitch is over and the demonstration (if any) is completed, the salesman then uses his previously exhibited order book as his closing technique. He asks for the customer's name, address, and so on, giving the impression that he regards the selling session as satisfactorily completed.

Still another salesman does not use the order book method. Instead he asks, at the appropriate time in the sale: "How do you want to pay? By check, credit card, or would you prefer that we bill you?" Note what the salesman does *not* say. He does *not* say, "Do you want to buy?" No real salesman ever uses this question because it permits the prospect to say no. Asking about the form payment should take is a favorite step of many salesmen. It is also a good closing form.

A commonly used closing technique favored by clothing salesmen and saleswomen is known as the "alteration" close. If the prospect is buying a suit or a dress or some other article of clothing that may require alterations, the closing step of the seller is, "Would you please wait just a moment while I get our fitter to see if any alterations are needed." Note what the salesman has done. He has assumed the sale is over and that the customer has accepted or has decided to buy the garment. This assumption puts the customer in the comfortable position of agreeing or the very uncomfortable position of saying no. You would be surprised at how many people will go along with the idea of buying. Sometimes, in speaking to friends, the buyer will say: "I bought this dress (or suit, or other garment) but I really don't know why. I was just looking around. I guess I can't resist a bargain." This is just a rationalization, of course. The answer is that the sale is completed because the salesman is well-prepared to make a sale, he knows all the steps in selling, and knows how to close the sale. The customer, on the other hand, is completely unprepared. No thought, or study, or human analysis is required on the part of the buyer. It's a fairly even contest though because the buyer has one word in his (or her) vocabulary that not too many salesmen can overcome. That word is no.

The Final Step—Closing the Sale

YOUR EMOTIONS

Your prospects have many emotions, some of which may show themselves during the time you are trying to make a sale.

What are some of these emotions?

They may be anger, annoyance, irritability, tenseness, an inability to concentrate on what you are saying, good humor, a relaxed feeling, loneliness, or possibly a tendency toward excessive conversation.

But consider that you may also have these characteristics and that your prospect may simply be reacting to the way you behave, talk, and think.

Therefore, an important factor in closing is your own emotional attitude toward closing. Now you may think you have a "poker face" and that no one could possibly know the way you feel, but you must at least give your prospect some credit for being perceptive. Thus, if you have any doubts about your ability to close a sale, you can be sure your prospect will know about it. This will instill some doubts into his mind about the item you are selling and will block your closing.

What does this mean then?

It would mean that in this instance the inability to close a sale isn't due to your prospect, but that the sale is being blocked by your own emotional attitude.

But what if you are angry, annoyed, tense, upset, disturbed or irritated. Aren't you allowed to have these very human emotions? Of course you are, but not during a sale. If you are angry, go away and do something else until your anger disappears or you have it under control. Customers will not buy from someone in an angry state of mind. A customer may be angry, annoyed, irritated, or tense and will buy while in such an emotional state, but *not* if the salesman is also angry, annoyed, irritated, or tense. The customer may have these emotions during a sale; the salesman may not.

TIME LENGTH OF SALES

No two sales take the same length of time. Some people make up their minds quickly, and are just as quick to place an order. Others dawdle, take their time, and often seem to have a feeling of complete indifference as to whether they buy or not. This means, then, that no two closing times are the same. You cannot insist that you will always start closing three minutes after the sale has started. The customer may be of the type who will let you close almost at once. With others you may need to take much longer. Thus, closing, like a sales pitch, must be completely flexible.

MOVING TOWARD THE CLOSE

For many years there has been a strong emphasis on the development of the "closing feeling" as a special condition for increasing sales.

What is this "closing feeling"?

It is simply a conviction on your part that you can close sales. Does this mean this feeling applies just to a single sale? No, it is a general feeling and means you know you can close sales with every prospect you have. It means the word "no" has been removed from your vocabulary as far as closings are concerned.

But how do you get this "closing feeling"?

The way to get it is to develop a closing technique. Nearly every good salesman develops his own methods of closing. This doesn't mean you should wait until you are confronted by a customer. Just as your sales pitch is previously prepared, you should be clear in your own mind, before selling, just how you are going to try to close.

Suppose your closing method isn't successful, what then? A good "close" isn't something you can stumble upon by accident the first time you try selling. It will take practice and selling experience. After you are unsuccessful in closing, think about what you did. Try to analyze your close. Was it too early? Was it too late? Was it the wrong approach? Did it offend the customer? What was the customer's reaction when you started the close? Did the customer give the impression of being pressured? Was the customer ready for the close? After you answer these questions, and probably some others you may have in mind, you will alter your close. This doesn't mean you will necessarily make drastic changes, for changes may not be required. You may just need to change your timing.

THE CLOSING CONVICTION

Is it necessary for you to have a positive technique and a positive feeling about closing? Yes, and for a simple reason. Closing is often just a state of mind. If you are sure you can close, and do so successfully, you will convey this feeling to your customer. This doesn't mean you are going to tell this to your customer. It will just be an attitude on your part, and because it has become a part of your mental make-up, will convey itself to your customer without words. You can be sure, however, your prospect will get the message.

Furthermore, since your confidence in your ability to close will be evident all the time you are talking to your customer, it will prepare him

You Can Become A Super Salesman

mentally to accept a close. The conviction that you can close will be transmitted to your prospect from the time you start your sales pitch to the moment you finish. It will be working for you all that time, silently but effectively.

Professional salesmen—men and women who have made a successful career in selling—are alert to the psychological advantage of this mental attitude and have used it, and are using it, to improve their own selling effectiveness.

A sales technique of this kind will increase your sales, and this will, in turn, increase your earnings. In addition, this will boost your confidence, which will also increase your sales.

HOW TO BUILD TRUST IN YOURSELF

If you can develop the attitude that your closing cannot fail, you will obtain two important selling advantages. Before we tell you about them, though, consider what it is we have asked you to do. We have asked you to develop a sales closing technique. We have asked you to polish it, revise it, improve it, and change it as you gain more experience. But in itself this isn't enough. A sales close is more than just a technique developed by a salesman. It must be accompanied by a particular frame of mind. The best close in the world will fail, even though it is properly developed and its timing is absolutely correct, if it is accompanied by a feeling of doubt or fear. The wrong mental attitude on the part of the salesman can spoil the best sales close.

Here are the two important advantages you will obtain, if you have the right mental attitude.

First, the right mental attitude will give you a feeling of trust in yourself. Consider this for a moment. If you are not convinced you can close a sale, how can you possibly convince someone else? In other words, you must sell yourself on your own ability. If you think you are a loser, you will be a loser.

But don't expect to be able to establish a feeling of trust in yourself overnight. It may take some time, depending on your own personality and your own belief in yourself. You must have faith in yourself before you can expect anyone else to do so.

Second, you will obtain the feeling of self-ability, something everyone else will notice, too. You won't be able to hide it, even if you wanted to, and there is certainly no reason for concealing it. Ultimately, this feeling of self-ability will work for you without your thinking about it. It will be automatic. It will "turn on" whenever you start a sale, and will do so without effort on your part. But, like everything else in life that is worthwhile, you can't get this important selling attribute by just wishing for it. It takes practice. It takes determination. It takes work. The rewards, though, are fantastic.

NERVOUSNESS IN SELLING

There are some salesmen and saleswomen who are nervous during the time they are trying to make a sale. There are a number of reasons for this. The sale may be very important to them from a financial viewpoint. They may be afraid of the customer. They may be worried about the possibility of failure. They may have doubts about their own ability. They may not have the necessary conviction about having the right technique for closing.

There is no doubt that such nervousness is a hindrance in making a sale. Your own attitude during a sale conveys itself to the prospect. If you are nervous, for whatever reason, you will make your sales prospect uneasy. He may not know why he feels this way, but the usual result is that he will try to cut your sales pitch short, may try to give you the minimum amount of his time, or may look for some excuse for ending the customer-salesman relationship.

EMOTIONAL CAUSES OF SELLING FAILURES

Why should the customer be concerned with or affected by a salesman's emotional attitude? The customer may not wish to become involved in someone else's problems. He may feel he is not getting the full benefit of the salesman's knowledge about the product. He associates the product with the salesman, and thinks that if the salesman is upset for some reason, then there must be something wrong with the product. The customer may also be afraid of having his own emotions aroused. The customer may be afraid that the salesman will lose complete control.

EXCUSES FOR EMOTIONALISM

But what if you have a valid reason for your emotion, whatever that emotion may be? Suppose you are nervous during a selling period. You may have personal problems. You may be facing some difficult decisions. Consider, though, that you aren't the only one to have such problems. In your profession a show of nervousness means more than in ordinary jobs where a personal conflict may have no meaning. You aren't the only person in the world with problems; however, in your case you may not show them.

What can you do then?

The best thing to do is to decide you are going to be calm and natural. You must use self-control. All through your sales pitch you are going to act as if the customer had already placed a firm order and was only trying to decide on certain technicalities, such as the quantity to order, delivery date, or a particular size or style. Is it easy? No. Must you do it? Yes.

Does this mean you are going to be acting a part? In a way, yes, but throughout our lives we all do some acting. In the presence of company invited to our homes we may often be on our best behavior. At home, without company, we may relax and behave in an entirely different manner. To be nervous during a sales pitch simply means you have decided to thrust the burden of your personal problems on to the customer.

Now look at it from your customer's viewpoint.

He has his own troubles and has no need of your, nor is he interested in sharing your problems, and there is no reason for him to do so.

Can you develop the necessary calm and assured attitude that professional salesmen have? That is up to you. Like anything else that is worthwhile, it takes practice. It takes determination and it requires courage, but it does separate the ordinary "order takers" from the professional salesman. It does separate those who are satisfied with a low income from those who are determined to get the good things in life. It certainly isn't impossible. The success of many salesmen proves it can be done. The only question is whether you want to make the effort.

It isn't something someone else can do for you. You must do it for yourself. But once you've accomplished it, no one can take it away from you. It's yours and will be yours for as long as you wish.

If you want to present facts about your product, you can only do so if you are in the proper mental frame of mind. Being angry, suspicious,

POSITIVE AND NEGATIVE ATTITUDES

There are two types of people.

The first group says, "I can do it" and the second says, "I can't do it." This sort of thinking applies to all human activities. If an individual has no faith in his own ability, who will believe in him?

A negative attitude—an attitude based on thinking of the "I can't do it" type—is automatically self-defeating. The phrase, "some people are their own worst enemies" is very true. People with a negative attitude work against their own success, against their own possible advancement, and in so doing keep themselves away from the possible rewards they might get for achievement.

A star salesman was the featured speaker at a recent convention. During his talk he supplied the audience with some of the secrets of successful salesmanship. Among other things, he said: "When I call on a prospect, I go in with the attitude that I have everything to gain and nothing to lose. If I leave the prospect without having made a sale, I am no worse off than I was before. It is true my total commissions haven't increased, but neither have they decreased. Yes, it is true I have lost some time, but even this isn't a complete loss, for the prospect has come to know me and I know more about him. I can use this knowledge the next time I go in to make a sale. And there is always the possibility that I will make a sale the next time, and so I make my pitch with optimism. I know that I can only gain, but I cannot lose."

This is a good approach in making any sales pitch. What have you got to lose? Nothing. What have you got to gain? Everything.

But why is it important or necessary to have the correct attitude when you talk to a prospective customer? The main reason is that your attitude and your outlook will communicate themselves to your prospect.

The Final Step—Closing the Sale

nervous, upset, irritated are all emotional characteristics that will prevent you from being factual.

IS NO THE ANSWER?

Probably the most frequently used word you will encounter in your selling work will be the word, "no." The reason for this is that many sales prospects take a defensive posture the moment they realize you are trying to sell them something. The prospect's first reaction is to say no.

But what does this word no mean?

It all depends on the sales prospect, his state of mind, and your state of mind. The no could be completely no, that is, under no circumstances will you be able to sell the prospect anything. There may be any number of reasons for this no. The prospect may not really be a customer. He may not have the money to buy what you are selling, nor does he foresee the likelihood of having any money in the near future. He may not be allowed to buy, that is, some other member of his family or his company may do all the buying. He may already be committed to some other salesman. He may be overstocked on the very items you are selling. He may have a previously built-up poor image of your product line.

It is important to understand the meaning of the prospect's no because some salesmen take the word "no" as a personal insult, or as a reflection on their ability as a salesman.

This is an emotional attitude. It means the salesman is unable to think in terms of facts, but is responding in terms of emotion. Keep in mind that every salesman often encounters the word no. You are no exception, and there is no reason why you should be. When a prospect says "no," he isn't saying or implying you are a poor salesman. The prospect may have a dozen other things on his mind. He may not even be paying much attention to you. The word "no" may be a purely defensive reaction on his part to give him time to think about what you are selling. There are all kinds of meanings to "no." There is the positively, I will not under any circumstances change my mind, no. There is also the I am not ready to buy at the present time no. There is also the I am not completely convinced no.

When the prospect says no it means you haven't as yet created a need on the part of the prospect to buy. Try to arouse or build that need. If you think the prospect has said no because of the cost of the product, call his attention to the money-saving features of the item you are selling. You can explain that the product will pay for itself. You can also explain that it will cost the prospect more by not buying. You can describe the economy features of your item.

The word "no" should also tell you something. It should tell you that you are far removed from a close. When a prospect says no, it is no time to take out your order pad and ask him when he wants delivery made. Thus, the words a prospect uses are an excellent guide to your closing pitch.

PREPARING FOR A "NO" ANSWER

The word "no" is your biggest hurdle. If you can get past it, your prospect is more likely to make a purchase.

What should you do when the prospect says no?

What you should really do is to prepare for that word well in advance. You can be sure this is the response you are going to get from some of your customers. What you should do is to be prepared with all the reasons that will prove "no" to be a poor argument on the part of the customer.

One successful salesman developed a technique that actually prevented the customer from ever saying no. During his sales pitch he watched the customer's facial and body gestures closely. As soon as he thought the customer was ready to say no, he countered with, "Now before you say no, let me show you . . ." and then went right into his sales pitch. By anticipating the customer, he deprived him of the force that the word no usually carries, and since the word no is the most effective one that can be used by any customer, he made his own selling job that much easier.

Still another successful salesman developed an excellent technique for getting over the hurdle of that first no. As soon as the customer said no, here is the way the salesman replied: "You've told me you don't want the product and I'm certainly not going to try to force it on you. But I know you're going to need it some day, so I'd like to take just a few minutes of your time to prove to you how our product can save money for you, each day, every day. Then, some day when you're ready to buy, you can come back and ask for me and I'll handle your order personally. Now here is what this product can do for you . . ."

Note what this salesman did. First, he did not accept no as an answer. Second, he calmed the fears of the prospect about making a purchase. Third, the salesman proceeded with his sales pitch just as though the prospect hadn't even mentioned the word no.

Here is what the salesman accomplished. He let the prospect register his protest against the sale. The salesman didn't argue with the customer, but made a reasonable appeal. He also brought up the point that the product could save money for the prospect. The ability to save money, without actually doing any extra work to save that money, has a strong appeal.

You Can Become A Super Salesman

ALTERNATIVE APPEALS

What if the product isn't one that could save money for the prospect? What if this powerful sales argument isn't available to you? This should present no problem. There are many other arguments you will have at your fingertips, if you've done your homework. All you need do is to select the most-wanted feature of the product. If, for example, you are selling cosmetics, your appeal can be a personal one. If you are selling high priced products, you can appeal to the vanity or snobbery of your customer. Whatever the product you are selling, it has some elements that have strong appeal, and that can result in sales. It is up to you to find those elements, to know them, and to use them.

SELLING SOUP

Are there some products that do not have built-in selling elements? No!

Every product has a built-in sales appeal, but it is up to you to find it. You must use your imagination. You must use your creativity. To understand more about what we mean by this, consider the case of two competing soup manufacturers. Manufacturer A sells a dehydrated soup. It comes in powder form and is available in small, flexible, plastic envelopes. To make soup using this product, all you do is heat some water, pour in the powder, and stir.

How does this manufacturer sell his product?

He doesn't.

He doesn't try to sell soup for a number of good reasons. His product doesn't look like soup, it doesn't smell like soup, and until it is mixed

The Final Step—Closing the Sale

with hot water, it doesn't taste like soup. And so what he does sell is convenience.

He knows there are a dozen other manufacturers, all trying to sell soup; soup in small cans; soup in large cans; soup with meat; soup without meat; and soup that will appeal to children. But the manufacturer of powder soup doesn't want to compete with them, and so what he sells is convenience. He emphasizes that you do not need to buy vegetables or meat. He emphasizes that all you need know is how to boil water. He emphasizes that his product need not be kept in a refrigerator, that it takes up little room, that you can take it with you to your office or factory, job, and that you can have soup wherever hot water is available. His product is just about as convenient as it can be. It will never spoil, and, to make the sales pitch even more convincing, manufacturer A says: "Water doesn't cost anything. We're not selling water. Why pay for something you can get for nothing? When you buy our soup that's exactly what you get. All soup. No water. And so our soup is the best food bargain your money can buy."

Note the double effectiveness of this sales pitch. The first element is convenience. The second element is economy. Both are very powerful arguments and are quite hard for competing manufacturers to overcome.

Now consider the manufacturer B. His soup is sold in cans. It takes up more room on supermarket shelves, on shelves in the home. It also costs more than powder soup. It would seem that manufacturer B has a serious selling disadvantage. Yet here is what he does. In his sales pitch he also emphasizes convenience. "With our soup," he claims, "you do not even need to add water. You need not worry about adding the right amount of water, because all our soups are scientifically balanced. When you prepare them they aren't too thin, or too thick. They are always just right. You can be an expert cook right in your own home. It's so easy, even a child can do it. No guessing. No experimenting."

Note the double effectiveness of this sales pitch: convenience and an appeal to the cooking instincts of the housewife.

Now you might think that nothing could be more ordinary than soup, and yet these two manufacturers have created a demand, a need, by looking beyond the fact that they sell soup. Neither one of them ever says, "Please buy our soup because it is a good soup." They don't even sell soup. They sell convenience, skill, or economy, or any other factor that will create a need, hence a demand, for their products.

HOW CAN YOU DO THIS?

It might seem easy to create a demand for soup but that's only because we explained the different techniques for you. No matter what product you are selling, there is always a method for selling it in a completely different way. Don't sell vacuum cleaners, sell cleanliness. Don't sell food freezers, sell the money to be saved by buying in bulk. Sell the idea that a freezer will pay for itself. Sell the thought that a freezer saves shopping time and money. Don't sell a television set, sell the convenience of sitting at home to watch movies. Sell the fact that most people, including neighbors, have bought this particular manufacturer's television set. Sell the idea of continuous, trouble-free enjoyment. Sell ease of operation—so simple even a child can bring in good pictures at any time. But don't sell a television set.

GUILT FEELINGS

Quite a few potential customers feel guilty about buying. They may not feel worthy, or they may think they do not deserve the product you are

The Final Step—Closing the Sale

selling. They aren't going to tell you this, for it may be they aren't even aware of their own feelings.

To overcome such thinking, you must make it easy for the customer to justify the purchase. A commonly used approach is: "It will save you money," or "We have just reduced the price but it will be sold at this price today only," or "You need this product for your health (or convenience)." "It will save you work." "It will save you time." You must make an appeal that the customer can use to overcome guilt feelings.

Here are some other suggested sales approaches for overcoming guilt feelings.

1. The product will help you keep your home cleaner.
2. Your family will appreciate it.
3. Your children need it.
4. It will make your home a more attractive place.
5. It will earn the gratitude (or respect, or admiration) of your husband (wife, child, and so on).

THE CLOSING AGAIN

How do you know when to close?

Close at the moment your customer gives an indication of willingness to buy. This willingness may be a word, a phrase, a sentence, a movement of the head, a smile, or a handshake. Watch for it, and then when you get it, close the sale.

You Can Become A Super Salesman

THE CUSTOMER'S SIGNALS

The customer's willingness to buy—your signal to close—will often come in the form of a question. Questions such as these indicate it is time to close:

1. Can I get it in a different color?
2. When can it be delivered?
3. I don't have enough money with me. Will you take a check?
4. Is the product warranteed?
5. Can I take it with me?
6. Can I get it gift wrapped?
7. Do I have to pay delivery charges?
8. Does it come with an instruction manual?
9. Is it sold on the installment plan?
10. If I make a deposit, will you hold the article for me?

These are just a few of the questions that could be asked by the customer that indicate the sale is over, and it's time to close.

But what if the customer doesn't ask a question? If the customer asks to try the product, if he examines it carefully, if he asks detailed questions about how the product works, if his facial expression changes when he operates the product, you have more than enough signals to indicate it is time to close.

TESTING FOR CLOSE

What if you aren't sure that it is the right time to close?

There are some prospects who are so close-mouthed, who are so

The Final Step—Closing the Sale

skilled at concealing their thoughts and feelings that you may not be able to detect any signals that will tell you whether to try for a close or not. A time-honored technique is to take out your order pad and ask for your customer's name and address. As you do, watch the reaction of the customer. If he supplies the information, then he is ready for the sales close. If he objects, or refuses to give his name and address, then closing is premature. The customer isn't ready.

ARGUMENTS AGAINST BUYING

Sometimes a prospective customer will begin to raise an entire series of objections against a product, and, oddly enough, this is just about time to close. Objections such as:

1. It's too big.
2. It's too small.
3. It isn't what I had in mind.
4. It costs too much.
5. I didn't expect to spend so much.
6. Can I get a discount?
7. It's too big for me to carry.
8. I don't think my husband (sister, wife, daughter) will like it.

What the customer may really be saying is: "Look. I think I'll buy it, but I need a little more information. I want to be assured I'm taking the right step." All you need to do now is supply that assurance, that bit of extra information, and the sale is ready to be closed.

You Can Become A Super Salesman

THE IMPORTANT WORD "WHY"

While the customer has a very powerful word at his disposal—the word no, some prospects go even further than that. They refuse to get involved in any discussion with a salesman. They think, and correctly so, that if there is no discussion, there can be no sale. What the salesman must do then is to "open them up," force them to talk. The best opener a salesman can use is the word "why." If a prospect says, "I'm not buying today," the salesman can ask, "why?" Note the salesman isn't really interested in the answer, he just wants the prospect to talk.

THE DEFERRED CLOSING

It isn't always possible to close. If you see that it is absolutely impossible to make a sale, then trying to close is useless, since it will lead to a definite no on the part of the prospect. If the prospect is one on whom you will call again, ending the sale with a strong no means your next selling effort to the same prospect will begin with a disadvantage. If you cannot close with an order, try to withdraw with the idea that the sale will continue some other day. In this way you will have an excuse for calling on the prospect again, and you will not be faced with a prospect who will say to you, "I told you no the last time and the answer is still no." You will at least have a chance at another time to continue to make your sales pitch and to determine the statement that will arouse a feeling of need in your customer for your product.

The Final Step—Closing the Sale

WHAT'S NEXT

We have said little about finding the customer, because we assumed the customer is in front of you and that you are about to begin your sales pitch.

That isn't always the case.

In door-to-door selling or in department store selling, there is no question of finding the customer. If the customer answers the door bell, there he is. If the customer stops when you demonstrate a product in a store, there he is. But there are many situations in which the salesman must first find the customer before he can begin his sales pitch.

Thus, in addition to all their other difficulties, some salesmen must first find their prospects and arrange to call on them before they have a selling opportunity. The next chapter tells you how to go about finding your customer.

FINDING THE CUSTOMER

You have developed a sales pitch, you have worked out a close that you think will work well, you know all the possible objections a customer might have, and you know all the answers. You know your product, its benefits, its advantages, and you are familiar with competing products as well. You still need one more element—a most essential one. You need customers!

If you are working in a store or if you are working door-to-door, you have no problem. In some selling arrangements the manufacturer will supply you with leads. These are responses obtained through magazine, radio, or television advertising. You may be assigned a certain territory and will be given all the leads from that area. Your job now will be to call on the prospects represented by the leads. You may call "cold," that is, you will visit the customers in their homes or places of business without making a previous appointment. Or, you may telephone them and arrange for a suitable time. In either event, you will be working with names that have been supplied to you.

In other selling setups, the company you represent may have an established selling route and will assign you to it. This route consists of customers who have previously made purchases from your company or who are prospects for doing so. Again, you will be supplied with a list of names. Equally important, you may also be given a "buying history," that is, a record of the customers' previous buying activities. The advantage here is that you will be working with established buyers, and you will have a better chance to sell. In this kind of situation, you may be accompanied by a more experienced salesman who will introduce you to the various customers and prospects.

FINDING CUSTOMERS

Not all salesmen are so fortunate to have someone supply them with a list of prospects or customers with a previous buying record. What do you do if you must find your own customers? You may have the best product in the world, and you may have considerable enthusiasm for it, but you must have customers. Customers will not look for you; you must find them. The problem is how. There are many techniques.

1. Finding a customer through recommendations. Speak to your family and to your friends. Let them know about the product you are selling. Ask them for the names of likely prospects. In some cases, to get started, a salesman may offer a small share of his commission to get names or may offer his product at a discount.

2. If your product is the kind that is used in the home, telephone people and ask for permission to use their home as a

demonstration center. In exchange for this privilege, offer a small payment or a commission on your sales or your product at a discount. The homeowner will then supply you with a list of names and telephone numbers you can use to arrange for the demonstration.

3. Every time you make a sale you will obtain a name and a phone number. Use these names in an effort to acquire new names. Try to encourage your customers to supply you with leads.

4. Get in touch with local community groups. Sometimes such groups will sponsor the sale of a product if they can earn some money from the sales. If they are agreeable to your offer, try to obtain their membership list and use that as the start of your own prospect list.

5. List your name and product on bulletin boards. Some local merchants have bulletin boards that are available without charge to customers. All you need to do is use your business card and a small description of the product you are selling. Other places that have bulletin boards are hospitals, old age homes, windows of local merchants, and so forth.

6. Use your telephone directory. Some salesmen make phone calls to learn if the phone subscriber is a possible prospect. You can use either the Yellow Pages, which lists companies according to their products or services, or the regular phone book, which often lists people according to their occupations.

7. City Directory. Your city may publish a directory listing the names, addresses, and occupations of the people living in that city. This directory, usually available at a low cost, can be used to get the names of prospective customers.

8. Social clubs. Such clubs are often interested in earning extra money or obtaining give away prizes. Contact the director of the

Finding the Customer

club, describe your product, and see if there is some way in which you can both benefit from your sales efforts.

9. Newspapers. Your local newspaper carries items of interest, a record of births, engagements, social events, new jobs, promotions, and names and addresses are usually given. Naturally, not all of these will be suitable prospects, but you should be able to find some that will be helpful.

10. You may be able to buy a previously prepared list of names from companies who specialize in making up such lists. To get such a list look in the Yellow Pages of your telephone directory for List Brokers. The cost of each name may be two or three cents each, but you may be required to buy in quantities of a thousand or more.

BUILDING YOUR PROSPECT LIST

This list of nine different ways in which to start your prospect list is just a beginning. As you make your calls, your prospect list will start to become smaller. Hence, it will be necessary for you to build up your list to keep it from disappearing altogether. There are a number of ways of doing this.

REFERRED LEADS

If your selling job is the kind in which you must find your own customers, the size of your prospect list will be uppermost in your mind. If you do make a sale, don't hesitate to ask your customer to give you as many names as possible of people who might be interested in buying your product. These names are known as *referred leads*. After you have the referred leads, ask your customer for permission to use his name. If he does not want to do so, do not insist. It is more important to have the names of prospects.

QUALITY OF LEADS

Not all leads will bring sales. Leads that bring a high number of sales are known as *quality or qualified leads*. A poor quality list is a list of names that results in little or no sales. A referred list of names is ordinarily of high quality.

Some salesmen who work door-to-door sometimes use a referred lead technique, either with permission or without. After calling on a prospect, they may visit an adjacent home and then mention the name of the neighbor they just called on. Sometimes they may add, "I've just visited your neighbor, Mr. ————, who suggested you might be interested in our new product." Salesmen sometimes copy names right from name plates on doors and use these as referred leads.

There are a number of different kinds of referred leads. Your present customer may telephone a new prospect for you and give you an introduction over the phone. Or else, the customer may give you a letter of recommendation to some of his friends or neighbors. In some cases he may hand you his business card and ask you to show it to the prospects he has supplied. In some instances he may visit a neighbor or friend with you and give you a personal introduction. Each of these is a referred lead, but they aren't all of the same quality. Probably the best is the personal introduction.

Finding the Customer

LEAD SPOTTERS

In an effort to gain more income, some people working as individuals or associated with some social group or a company will supply leads to salesmen. These so-called *lead spotters* receive a small commission from the salesman upon the successful conclusion of a sale. It represents a sort of "finders fee".

GETTING LEADS BY MAIL

Some salesmen use literature and form letters supplied by the companies they represent in an effort to obtain customers. The letter and literature combination is a preliminary sales effort. It should be accompanied by a prepaid return envelope so that the prospect has no expense in contacting the salesman. Frequently, in such mailings, the prospect is encouraged to make a collect call. It may be necessary to mail to a hundred people or more to get a single quality lead. Whether or not the effort and expense is worthwhile depends on what you are selling and its cost. It is difficult to use this technique with low-priced items, since the cost of mailing and followup may be more than the profit to be made from the sale.

SELLING BY BUSINESS CATEGORY

Your product may be suitable for all people or it may be used only by a restricted group. If, for example, you are selling an item that can only be used by plumbers, then your prospect list is ready and waiting for you in the classified section of the phone book. You can also buy a previously prepared list from a list broker. If your product is one that is sold to educators, school teachers, and school principals, you can get a list of prospects from a list broker, a teacher's union, magazines that have teachers as subscribers, or by going from school to school.

FAIRS AND CONVENTIONS

Still another way of selling your product is to take booth space in fairs and conventions. Of course, you must select a fair or convention that will bring in potential buyers who would be interested in what you are selling. If you are selling electric ranges for use in the home, taking booth space in an automobile show will be of no help. Arrange for space in a home-makers show, or a home appliances show, or a "home" show. Sometimes the manufacturer of the product you are selling will do this and will ask you to act as his representative at the show. A commonly used technique of getting a large list of prospect names during a show is to offer a prize of some kind. All the people visiting your booth are invited to register by writing their names and addresses on previously prepared cards. These cards are used for a "draw" in which selected names will be eligible for prizes.

This "register" technique is also used by companies when a prospect walks in off the street and indicates his interest in the company's product. The name may be given to a salesman who works in-house and may then be turned over to another salesman for follow-up, if the original salesman did not make a sale.

Finding the Customer

THE FREE SAMPLE METHOD

Still another technique for getting names of prospects is to send an offer, possibly to a list of names obtained from a telephone directory, offering a free product of some kind. All that is required of the prospect is that he furnish his name and address on a prepaid postcard enclosed with the offer. The sample, of course, is not mailed to the prospect but is delivered in person by the salesman. The free product, a premium, may consist of a small notebook, ballpoint pen with the prospect's name engraved on it, or some similar item, and is used to help build a prospect list. This method works well because there are so many people who cannot refuse something that is "free."

THE CONTEST TECHNIQUE

To get names a company will sometimes sponsor a contest. The contest may be nothing more elaborate than a simple sentence to be made up, such as "I like the XYZ product because . . ." with an answer of 25 words or less. The names of those entering the contest form a prospect list. This method is generally used by a company anxious to supply its selling staff with names.

NAMES AND LOCATION

If you are selling in a small area, such as a particular city or county, names of people who live hundreds of miles away will be of no value. You can either discard such names if you get them, or work a "swap" arrangement with other salesmen who handle your own product line but

You Can Become A Super Salesman

who live in these other areas. A prospect's name must not only have "quality," that is, be a good lead that is worth developing, but it must also be a suitable lead, that is, located where you can meet the prospect.

SOME DO'S AND DON'TS FOR SALESMEN

It would be impossible to tell you everything you should or should not do in selling, since a lot of what you need to know can only be acquired through on-the-job experience. But there are some points we can tell you about that can have a considerable effect on your selling success.

1. Don't touch your customer. Yes, there are some selling jobs, such as in the clothing trades where it is necessary to do so. Some salesmen, however, think nothing of draping an arm over the shoulders of the prospect, or pulling the prospect toward them by grabbing the lapels of a suit, or putting one hand on or around a shoulder. Many customers find this familiarity offensive, and it is. Shake hands with the prospect, *if* the prospect seems inclined to do so, otherwise, don't.

2. Don't try to tell funny stories. The "funny story" selling technique has been outdated for many years. You are a salesman, not a comedian. Your job is to sell, not amuse or entertain the customer. Yes, some salesmen buy theatre tickets for prospective customers, but they allow professional actors to do the entertaining.

3. Don't ever make remarks about religion. This is a sensitive subject and has no place in selling. It cannot possibly help you make a sale, but it can cause your customer to walk away.

4. Don't make disparaging remarks about the competition. All you need do is to emphasize the superiority of your own product. Let

the customer draw his own conclusions. After all, you may be working for the competition some day.

5. Don't make any remarks about race. This is a free country and you're entitled to your opinions. This does not give you the right to make any remarks, good, bad, or indifferent about race. Again, you are a salesman, not a teacher of social studies.

6. Don't talk about politics. No matter what your political beliefs may be, keep them to yourself. If the customer brings up the subject, listen to him, but add nothing to this phase of the conversation. Do not wear any lapel pins or buttons that will identify you with any group of any kind. Some people use the power to buy as the power to punish. They like to boycott salesmen whose views do not agree completely with their own.

7. Can you talk about the weather? Yes, briefly, unless you are selling weather vanes, thermometers, barometers, anemometers, and so on. Discussion of the weather should be short and is of value only because it "breaks the ice" and gives the customer-salesman relationship a chance to get started.

8. Should you mention your own personal problems? Never.

9. What if the customer brings up his own personal problems? Listen and then as tactfully and gracefully as possible and steer the conversation back to the product you are selling. You are a salesman, not a healer of broken hearts, damaged lives, and twisted spirits.

10. What about an occasional drink? No. The main reason is not because alcohol will slow you down in your work, although it can, but because it will make your breath offensive. Many people like the odor of liquor, but not from the mouth of a salesman. Also, stay away from garlic, onions, and other foods that

You Can Become A Super Salesman

advertise themselves vigorously. Make sure your breath is fresh and clean.

11. Should I chew gum while selling? No, not even if you are a gum salesman.

12. Can I sit down while selling? Only if you are invited to do so by the customer. When calling on a customer and the customer is seated, wait for the customer to ask you to sit down. You acknowledge your customer as your host. This is an act of politeness many customers appreciate.

13. You are calling on a prospect and want to telephone another prospect to find out if he is in and will see you. Should you use the phone, provided you ask for permission to do so? No. Don't use your customer's premises as your business office. Wait until you are outside and then use a pay phone. While many people will not refuse the use of their telephone, they may resent being asked.

14. Should you smoke while selling? No.

15. You are making a sale and while doing so are informed by another salesman that you have a phone call. What should you do? Ask the other salesman to get the number of the calling party. Don't interrupt your sale. If you do, you will probably lose the customer. If the call is important, the other party will wait for you. If it isn't important, you will have lost nothing.

16. Some salesmen feel it is good psychology to make a customer wait before attending to them and that it puts the salesman in a dominant position. How is this as part of a selling technique? Terrible.

17. You have a customer who keeps interrupting your sales pitch. What should you do about this? Listen.

Finding the Customer

18. You have a customer who keeps asking you to repeat what you have said. What should you do? Repeat what you have said, speak more slowly, and speak more clearly. You may need to speak louder. Some customers have a hearing problem that they refuse to acknowledge.

19. You have a customer who keeps praising a competing product. What should you do? This is a customer technique known as "salesman baiting." He is just trying to get you to lose control of yourself. Answer his statements with facts about your own product.

20. You have a customer who claims, falsely, that he can buy your product elsewhere at a much lower price. Emphasize the fact that you are a one-price store; let the customer know that the sales price is fixed by the manufacturer; ask the customer if the so-called lower price applies to the model you are selling; find out if the so-called lower price applies to a used or damaged product. Sometimes a store or salesman will sell at a lower price to clear store-worn merchandise or goods that have been partly damaged in transit.

21. What should you do if you are trying to sell to a prospect who is constantly bothered by small children while you are making your sales pitch. Be patient.

22. What if a customer asks you, as a personal favor, to cash a check for him? Tell him you are unable to do this. Refer him to the store's credit department. If you are not working for a store, but are an independent salesman, you have a very short but excellent word you can use. No.

23. What do you do if a customer becomes abusive? Do not answer.

24. Should you keep a record of your sales? Of course.

25. Is it true that the more calls a salesman makes the more sales he

makes? Generally, yes. If the leads are qualified leads, and if the salesman is serious about his work, it is true that more calls mean more sales.

26. Do all sales take the same amount of time? No.

27. What should you do if a customer offers you some "money under the table" to get a better discount? Turn it down for two very good reasons. The first is that it is dishonest, and the second is that you should not sell your professional career for the small amount of money involved.

28. A customer fails to keep his appointment with you. What should you do? Make another appointment.

29. You have an appointment to meet a customer but are delayed. What should you do? Phone the customer and explain the reasons for the delay.

30. A customer complains to your employer that you cheated him during a sale. What should you do? Show your employer your sales slip or your selling record.

DEVELOP YOUR MEMORY

Many salesmen, who are otherwise mediocre, have good sales records because of one factor in their favor. They have good memories. A good memory, though, is acquired, not inherited. If you are given a customer's name, remember it. Here are some points that should help you.

1. When you are introduced to the customer, mention his name. As you do this, look at the customer so that you associate his name with his features.

Finding the Customer

2. Mention the customer's name several times during the sales pitch. This will have two benefits. It will help you remember the customer's name, and it will make him listen to you more carefully. Mentioning someone's name is an excellent method of fixing his attention.
3. If the customer hands you his business card, read the customer's name out loud. Don't worry. The customer won't object.
4. As you write the customer's name on your sales order form, repeat it out loud.

There is a great advantage in knowing a customer's name. During repeat sales, it is helpful to greet the customer by name as he approaches you. Smart restaurant operators (yes, they are salesmen, too) always try to learn the names of their customers and to greet them personally.

What if you have dozens and dozens of customers? Should you be able to remember all their names? Yes, if you can do so. After all, you aren't being asked to memorize dozens and dozens of names at the same time; you learn them one at a time.

DEVELOP YOUR ARITHMETIC

There is nothing more embarrassing than filling out an order form and making a mistake in arithmetic. This not only creates a bad impression on your customer but may give him the mistaken impression you are trying to cheat him. Arithmetic used in selling is simple and is taught in the elementary grades. You should be able to add, subtract, and take discounts. You may also need some basic multiplication. If this is one of your weak points, practice. It isn't difficult, all it takes is some effort. If you don't enjoy doing arithmetic, don't worry about it, you have plenty of company.

You Can Become A Super Salesman

DEVELOP LEGIBILITY

Some people have a handwriting that cannot be deciphered by anyone, including themselves. Don't scribble or scrawl. If you do indeed write poorly, then print. Make sure the customer's name and address and phone number are legible. Make sure the product, its price, discount, and sales tax, if any, are perfectly clear. Make sure the total price is neatly written. In short, the entire order or sales slip must be written in such a way that it can be read by anyone. Above all, make sure your name, or employee number, or other code used to identify you is also clear. You do want to get credit for the sale, don't you?

DEVELOP RESPONSIBILITY

Some people are born losers, but only in the sense that they lose things. They lose umbrellas, attache cases, wallets, purses, loose change, orders, sales slips, product samples, and so on. This is such a common condition that some manufacturers insist on getting a deposit for samples, which is refundable when the samples are returned. Losing things is often just a bad habit. It can be disastrous for a salesman.

DEVELOP YOUR LISTENING ABILITY

Nearly all of us think much faster than we talk. As a result, there is a natural tendency to think of other things when a customer is talking. We

Finding the Customer

may be thinking of counter arguments, our sales pitch, or topics not associated with the sale or the product. During this time, however, the customer may be saying something that is important as far as the sale is concerned. Therefore it is imperative to be a 100 percent listener, not a half listener.

When a customer is talking, concentrate on what he is saying; don't daydream and don't let yourself become distracted by other people talking, a radio playing, or someone's phone conversation.

DEVELOP CORRECT GRAMMAR

Some customers find errors in grammar extremely irritating. Here are some common mistakes.

Incorrect	*Correct*
I don't have no . . .	I don't have any . . .
Him and me . . .	He and I . . .
We don't never . . .	We don't ever . . .
We ain't . . .	We aren't . . .
Them three articles . . .	Those three articles . . .

These are just a few examples out of the hundreds of possible errors, but don't worry, no one makes them all. But if someone does correct your grammar, they are doing you a favor. If you feel that correct speech is your weak point, there are a number of things you can do about it. There are many books on the subject, which you can buy or borrow from your local library. Many communities give adult education courses; a course in correct speech would be a tremendous advantage.

You Can Become A Super Salesman

DEVELOP DECISION-MAKING ABILITY

Not all customers need to be sold. Sometimes all a customer needs to be able to do, in order for you to close a sale, is to make a decision. "What size should I get, style, color?" "When should I get it delivered?" "Do I want it gift wrapped?" "Should I buy more than one?" "Should I pay cash or by check?" "Should I get the budget model or the deluxe unit?"

Note, there is no question about whether or not to make a purchase. When a customer asks questions like these, or questions similar to these, then the problem is one of helping the customer make a decision. At this time, the customer wants you to help him make a decision. This is not the time for you to stand back in a detached manner insisting, in effect, that the customer make up his (or her) own mind. Some customers just can't do that. They may be in the habit of evading responsibility. They may want someone to share the responsibility. They may regard you as an authority on the subject of your product. Whatever the customer's reason may be, you can now close the sale by joining with the customer in the decision-making process.

DEVELOP YOUR PRODUCT KNOWLEDGE

Sometimes a salesman is involved with selling a tremendous number of small items and so may not be in a position to know them all well. To overcome this, try studying the manufacturer's catalog; become familiar, at least, with those items that move most rapidly.

Some manufacturers cooperate with a salesman by offering sales seminars. These are useful ways in which to learn more about the product line because it gives you a chance to ask questions. If you have the

Finding the Customer

opportunity, take a guided tour through the manufacturer's plant. Some manufacturers make such tours available for salesmen to let them see just how the product is produced.

Some salesmen also learn more about products in an unusual way. They keep records of their customers and, after a period of time, phone them to learn something about the performance of the product. In this way they learn the strengths and weaknesses of the item they are selling.

Still another way of learning more about your product and its market is to subscribe to trade magazines. Just about every product manufactured has a trade magazine, which includes descriptions of the products, competing products, new products, and marketing and selling conditions. Such magazines are excellent sources of prospect leads.

DEVELOP YOUR INDUSTRY KNOWLEDGE

It will also be helpful if you develop your knowledge of the entire industry in which your product is involved. If, for example, you are involved in selling refrigerators, you should be concerned with the home appliance market. It is true that refrigerators are just one type of home appliance, but you should have more than just a narrow outlook. Knowing about the entire market will give you a better perspective about how your product relates to all others. It may also give you some valuable selling ideas.

DEVELOP YOUR PROSPECT LIST

One of the best ways of getting new sales prospects is the "customer get a customer" technique in which a satisfied customer gives you the names of several people who might be interested in your products. Always be alert for other methods. Whatever you read, wherever you go, every time you sell, always keep in mind you really have a double job—selling and finding new prospects for sales. You can sell only as long as you have people to buy. One enterprising salesman of baby products always watched birth announcements in newspapers, sent a card of congratulations, and then followed up a day or two later with a house call. Some salesmen make arrangements with maternity floors in hospitals to be supplied with lists of names of new mothers, but this isn't always possible. Names of newly engaged couples or social activities of married couples, printed in newspapers, are often suitable prospects for a variety of products. One alert salesman of store burglary alarm systems always called on stores that were victims of a burglary—information readily obtained from his newspaper.

DEVELOP YOUR ABILITY TO EVALUATE PROSPECTS

It's a rare salesman who hasn't fallen into the trap of going through an elaborate sales pitch, only to learn that the prospect either has no money or else does not have the authority to buy. If you have a number of products in various price lines, you should try to determine the price range interest of your prospect. If you are selling to someone in a business, make sure the person you are talking to has the authority to make the purchase. A simple statement such as, "I've been told you're the buyer for XYZ Company." "I've been anxious to meet you for some time since I think we're in a good position to save you quite a bit of money." At this point the prospect may or may not show interest, but will ask the salesman to continue, or he may break in with, "Well, I guess I'm not really the person you should see. The man who does our

Finding the Customer

buying is Mr. ————." In some companies the buyer is so essential that he is given a separate office with a title, generally Buyer, printed across a door or window.

As far as the spending ability of your buyer is concerned, some salesmen lead right off with, "Could you give me some idea of the price range you have in mind?" One real estate salesman uses this approach and then softens what may seem to be a hard question with, "I just didn't want to waste your time looking at some houses that are priced right out of the market." Here the salesman is doing two things: He is getting information concerning the amount of money the prospect is willing to spend, and he is also telling them that some houses are too high priced and he does not approve of this. Quite naturally this will arouse a sympathetic reaction from his prospect.

DEVELOP YOUR SALES PITCH

If you find your sales are on the downgrade, if you feel you are running into more and more customer sales resistance, consider the fact that your sales pitch may have outlived its usefulness. No sales pitch lasts forever. Some salesmen, originally burning with energy and ambition, develop a sales pitch that works successfully for quite some time, but times change and people change. The trouble is, though, that it is difficult for a salesman to let go of a sales pitch that has proved its usefulness. The salesman becomes afraid, and the more fearful he becomes, the tighter he holds on to his sales pitch. He starts to blame everything except the one thing that may be holding him back. The product isn't what it used to be; the manufacturer is beginning to price himself out of the market; competition is getting tougher; customers are becoming more demanding.

You Can Become A Super Salesman

Develop a good sales pitch, but don't look on it as final or permanent, sooner or later it must change.

DEVELOP SELLING AIDS

Not all salesmen rely solely on a verbal sales pitch. Some make use of charts and graphs. Some salesmen develop various kinds of visual aids. Some use slide projectors. It all depends on what you are selling and the kind of sales audience you have. If your products are the kind that are helped by "props," develop them. Find out what selling devices other salesmen are using for similar products. Become a prospect for sales aids. Some salesmen give away premiums as a means of introducing themselves to prospects. One salesman carries an easel with him and a previously prepared set of charts in attractive colors. Some salesmen sell with the help of wall charts, others use portable tape players.

DEVELOP YOUR OPENING STATEMENT

Your opening statement—the first words your prospect hears from you—will often determine the entire course of the sale. Your opening statement may cause the prospect to become hostile, resentful, and determined not to buy, or, at the other extreme, it may make him feel he has found a friend. A store salesman, opening with, "Good morning, sir. May I help you?" has a much better approach than, "Anything you want?" Never ask a customer if he wants to buy something. It is up to you to assume that he does indeed want to buy something.

There are many different kinds of opening statements. One salesman starts by asking his door-to-door customers if they will answer a few questions for him for a survey he is making for his company. Another salesman shows his prospect two items and asks his customer if he can recognize which is the standard brand. The whole idea of an opening statement is to break down the reserve of the prospect, to remove suspicion on the part of the prospect, and to establish a friendly atmosphere. This is quite a lot to accomplish in just a few seconds. The approach you use will vary, depending on what you are selling and your customer. One salesman calling on buyers in a factory starts with, "I'd like to show you how we can save your company $———— a year." Every businessman and every buyer is interested in saving money, and so this salesman gets right to the heart of the matter. The same salesman, selling a product to a housewife might say, "I would like just a few minutes to show y⅔ how I can save you hours of housework." In each case the appeal is made to the self-interest of the consumer. The salesman must also give the impression of being friendly, helpful, pleasant, and easy to get along with. While the salesman can learn much from his customer's appearance and attitude, you can be sure the prospect is "sizing up" the salesman and deciding whether to let the conversation continue.

TIME YOUR SELLING

People will be more inclined to buy when you do not interfere with their daily routine. A prospect about to go out to lunch may have neither the time nor the inclination to listen to you. This means the number of hours during the day that are "effective" selling hours are limited. This also means you must make the most of them. The only way to do this is to plan your day, before you start, not during. Some successful salesmen plan their selling activities the night before. If their selling job involves calling on customers, they will arrange a route that will consume the least traveling time, enabling them to make the maximum number of calls. This is advantageous when calling "cold," that is, without a previous appointment.

Follow the same procedure when calling on customers with whom you have made appointments. The problem here is that you may not know in advance just how much time each sale will take. Hence, when making such appointments, try to get the prospect to agree to be flexible about the time. If this isn't possible, you will have to develop "time sense." In other words, you will have to allow yourself a definite amount of time for each sale.

CHECK YOURSELF

There is nothing more frustrating than for a salesman to find himself unprepared. If you sell electrical appliances, make sure the appliance is in working order before you are surrounded by prospects invited to attend a demonstration. Make sure you have your order book and that you can find it at once, not by scrambling through miscellaneous papers, catalog sheets, or other odds and ends. Don't ever put yourself in the embarrassing position of having to ask your prospect for the loan of a pen so you can enter his order. Be sure to carry at least one pen as a spare.

If it is part of your selling technique to supply the prospect with printed information, make sure you have it with you. When you forget printed information and then offer to mail it, it is a bad way to do business.

If you must make some kind of presentation involving various materials, not only make sure you have them, but that you have them arranged in the order in which you want to present them. The clue to a

Finding the Customer

successful sales presentation is the smoothness and ease with which it moves from start to finish. If you are required to show samples, have these samples available so that you can get at them quickly, without unpacking the entire contents of a sample case.

BE PROFESSIONAL

Selling is an art and a skill, but to be a professional, you must think and act like one. This means knowing your product line, knowing the product line of the competition, understanding yourself, understanding your customers, and developing all the personal qualities that will make you a supersalesman. Anyone can become a super salesmen—all that is necessary is an intense desire to be one.